The Preacher-Prophet
in Mass Society

The
Preacher-Prophet
in
Mass Society

by Jesse Jai McNeil

William B. Eerdmans Publishing Company
Grand Rapids, Michigan

PRINTED IN THE UNITED STATES OF AMERICA

INTRODUCTION

When in April of this year the author first mentioned his intention to develop in book form the substance of lectures given at the Michigan Pastors' Conference in January of 1961, I rejoiced both for future readers of these creative addresses as well as for the deserved recognition which the author himself should have in his developing ministry. The fortunate continuation of addresses given at the Michigan Pastors' Conference at the University of Michigan with others added when the author lectured at Virginia Union University School of Religion and in ministers' institutes in California and Texas on the same basic subjects, brings together in small book form materials of essential concern not only to every preacher but to individual Christians who are searching their souls for individual and social ethical standards and how to keep imagination and conviction warm in their own mind and spirit.

Before the reader enters into the serious reading of the six chapters, a word about the author will provide some living interpretation of the ideas and conceptions which have been expressed. Jesse Jai McNeil himself has been an outstanding "preacher-prophet" in the Tabernacle Baptist Church of bustling Detroit for many years. A man of keen intellect and quiet, simple spirit, he is being recognized as one of the great preachers of our time, speaking from the heart of God to the heart of the people of our generation. The reader quickly realizes him to be a man of God, a keen observer of human life, an able interpreter of mass society in one of the great mass industrial centers of the world. At every point, he proves himself to be a scholar, not only in his ability to handle interpretations of the Bible but likewise in handling situations with which psychology and sociology aptly deal. His ability to discern the problems of the industrial masses and to struggle intelligently in a discriminating way with the ethical and religious implications of these problems is noteworthy. Above all, he is a true orator who warms the truth with living, creative energy. No man could have all these qualities and not be a man of many parts; and that is exactly what Dr. McNeil is. He is a minister of souls, an author of real ability, a technician able to use every normal device to present the truths which he thinks in the language and point of view of the listener, and he is a democratic worker with his peers on important committees of his church denomination and with the National Council of Churches.

One of the college songs of my Alma Mater included the phrase "Old yet forever new." Thousands of articles and books have been written about the preaching of the Word of God. Yet this subject can always be fresh and new when the seers of the pulpit come alive in their generation to speak God's word and use the symbols with contemporary motivation. Chapter 1 brings an important message on the need for the prophet-preacher to have the profoundest view of man and a deep understanding of the condition under which his fellow men so easily in our society live "hollow" and "dying" lives. When he raises the question of how the preacher-prophet today conceives of his own calling, life, and ministry, the author is dealing with a subject which every preacher should read, reread, and think through in view of his own convictions and his personal relationship to the life-giving source of his preaching.

Chapter 2 again goes to the heart of the matter when Dr. McNeil declares "the authenticity of his calling is proved by the miracle it performs during every act of true preaching." The reader quickly realizes that this miracle is within the preacher himself as well as in the feelings created in the minds of those who listen.

The keen analysis of the distinction between culture and civilization in Chapter 3 forms a basis for understanding why today religion is an indispensable integrant of group and personal life. It likewise provides an interpretation of why there is such a disparity between what is preached as the Christian faith and what is possible in the present set of circumstances under which man lives in mass society. Dr. McNeil well points out that it is through participation in the making of moral decisions that the preacher-prophet helps "mass men" to know what they can do in a particular concrete situation. Every preacher would do well to study what the author has to say about the three basic urges to which the gospel today must appeal, namely, the urge *to do* (activity), the urge *to belong* (community), and the urge *to be* (authenticity).

The author rises to a height of sound thinking in his consideration in Chapter 4 of "God's Voice in Community Affairs." His basic illustration of how the wandering clans of Israel had ordered their lives according to a *mishpat*, which was not only well suited to nomadic life but which was founded upon principles of enduring values, provides a scriptural basis for understanding the long line of the development of the ethic which came to its flower in Jesus Christ. In his challenge to preachers today to have greater concern in community affairs, he says, "he will find no concrete social programs to offer the community, but there will be challenge and inspiration aplenty in this Book for the collective achievement of justice, public order and love." "There is a Chinese proverb which says that there are five and not four points on a compass: north, south, east, west, and *the point where you are*. So we ourselves are important in working our way out of any problem whatever it is."

The last two chapters, "The Word of God — with Imagination" and "The Word of God — with Conviction," add to and enrich with illustration and suggestion the main thesis developed in all of the addresses. Typical of his preaching, Dr. McNeil correctly includes quotations throughout his addresses from the scriptures to warm the hearer with repetition and to awaken him with keenly directed arrows. As a friend and as the Ann Arbor chairman of the program committee of the Michigan Pastors'

Conference where several of these chapters were delivered as addresses, I would take the liberty to suggest that here is a book which should be constantly in the pastor's study, a book to which reference can be made again and again as the spirit or insight or imagination of the preacher needs rekindling.

DeWitt C. Baldwin
Co-ordinator of Religious Affairs

University of Michigan
Office of Religious Affairs
Ann Arbor, Michigan

PREFACE

The substance of this book was presented first as a series of lectures at the 1961 Michigan Pastors' Conference at Ann Arbor, Michigan, upon invitation of the University of Michigan and the Michigan Council of Churches. It has been subsequently presented at a number of Ministers' institutes across the country.

Encouragement to put this material into book form has come to the author from a considerable number of ministers and pastors, as well as from his publisher. This he has done not because he feels that his discussion of the preacher-prophet is in any way unique but simply to accent the urgent and continuing concerns of many men who have answered the call to the Christian ministry and to give his own personal testimony of its demands, its privileges, and its power.

If the concerns of the Christian minister and the ministry into which he has been called have been stated in a way which will bring more vividly and poignantly to some the challenges to our ministry of the condition of mass man, and if it be found that some different materials are used here to point up these concerns and challenges which at the same time may guide some of the author's readers to make serious use of a source of material which they have not hitherto employed, then he will feel that another book on this subject treated here may not be without some real purpose and value.

The quality of this work has been considerably improved by the competent scrutiny and sound suggestions of Dr. Allan A. Zaun, minister of the Jefferson Avenue Presbyterian Church, Detroit, Michigan. Dr. DeWitt Baldwin, Director of Religious Affairs of the University of Michigan, has read this work in its entirety and has honored the author by consenting to write the Introduction to it. The author is sure that this work is a better book because of Dr. Baldwin's highly valued contribution to it. He also feels the certainty that the work done here, as well as his previous efforts, reaches the reader greatly improved in quality because of the close and continued assistance he receives from his wife, Pearl, his kindest and most acute critic. To all three of these ministers of Christ in their respective vocations — fellow laborers all in the cause of Christ — he acknowledges his debt.

The author also expresses his gratitude to Mrs. Lois Rowlett and Mrs. A. Louise Jones for their care, accuracy and efficiency in preparing the typescript for submission to his publisher and to all the publishers listed in the Bibliography who have granted kind permission to quote from the sources of which they are the copyright owners.

Let God be praised for all those who lovingly and willingly share the inglorious labors of a witness to Him and a service to many through the printed word.

C O N T E N T S

CHAPTER ONE

Challenge to a Self-Portrait

The preacher-prophet today is one with the prophets of old in the personal and spiritual demands made upon him as a champion of the ways of God in the society to which he belongs. Regardless of the nature of his particular society, the personal and spiritual demands remain the same. The preacher-prophet is at once an alien and a citizen in the most existential sense of these terms. God has chosen him not only to tell the people what they *ought* to do, but also to live and persistently to proclaim His message on the basis of this "oughtness." Being and championing what ought to be is in a very real sense being a citizen of the future and living in this future. Yet while the preacher-prophet represents a citizenship of the future, he must live the life of the present. For the present belongs to God as well as does the future. And there can be no future if he scorns the present and withdraws from it. With idealistic eyes and realistic feet he must champion the ways of God and discern what is possible and achievable in the everyday affairs of mortal, sinful, mass man.

I

This study gives attention to three major questions which should be of the utmost concern to the preacher-prophet today. The first of these questions is: How can the preacher-prophet be an effective harbinger of the ways of God in the society to which he and his fellow dying men belong if he does not under-

13

stand the times in which he lives? This understanding is essential to his message and work. But it need not be contingent upon the availability to him and his possession of all the facts or knowledge centering around and emerging from the technical research of our modern scientific pursuits. He will not need to know the processes involved in splitting an atom or in making a hydrogen bomb or an IBM missile to understand how fatally destructive any of these may be in the hands of demonic men. Neither does he need to presume that he has the knowledge to advise the government on how much of a stock pile of the various weapons of war is enough for the protection of our borders or as a deterrent to an aggressive enemy. He does not need this presumption of knowledge to understand or to declare the futility of armed might. His understanding of the times will come partially from the profound and acute analyses and interpretations of the facts of our times by competent observers, researchers and experts in many fields. But the depth of his understanding will come from the spiritual insights which belong to those who are both sensitive to the operation of the laws of God in the world of men and nature and receptive of the revelation God chooses to make of Himself "at sundry times and in divers manners."

In other words, the understanding of the times which is essential to the message and work of the preacher-prophet is not based on the technical knowledge which only a limited number of highly and specially trained men and women may acquire in mass society, but on an understanging of man, the mortal, sinful, but godlike creature, in his relation to the potential power of the things he may possess or with which he may become allied.

The understanding which the preacher-prophet must possess — and in which he must excel — is that understanding which informs him of what the people ought to do in response to any given demand or challenge of our common life. Moreover, this is an understanding not of what people will do but of what they ought to do; that which is morally right and possible. This is the preacher-prophet's realm and the burden of his message. In this realm he can never be effectively assailed. Under the burden of this message he never becomes a false prophet because of his presumptive intrusion into a realm of thought and authority which is alien to him. With this understanding of his task, he may be grieved by the unresponsiveness of the people to his message but he is not disillusioned by it, nor does he despair because of it. His understanding of the times is that of knowing what the people *ought* to do and not what they with promptitude of spirit and gratitude of heart, because of his sincere concern for them, *will* do.

God, through His Holy Spirit, is the source of the knowledge and wisdom which the preacher-prophet possesses concerning the times. God reveals to him, sometimes through the written Word and the events of history and sometimes through the direct and immediate knowledge of intuition, the paths He takes and the bounds He has set in the affairs of men. "The worldly hope men set their hearts upon" turns to ashes or prospers under the providential will and care of God for man. His will and care are reflected alike in His judgment upon the values and ends which man seeks and to which man would pledge his fealty.

II

A second question with which this study will be concerned is that of the problem of communicating with mass man: How can the preacher-prophet communicate effectively to his modern hearers if he does not understand the man to whom he must address the Word of God today? Can he take it for granted that the man with whom he must establish communication in order to proclaim the saving deed of God in Christ Jesus is the same as man has always been? How does the gospel come to man in mass society? If the preacher-prophet condemns sin before his modern-day hearers, should he stop short of an interpretation of sin which, while not conforming to the preachments of other years, may have more meaning to the hearer today? For how long will his listeners be content to listen to him without becoming restive, notwithstanding his message of life and death? How patient can he expect his hearers to be with a proclamation

(!) which lacks the stamp of personal conviction and sincerity, relevancy and vitality? Must he compete with those whose aim is to entertain the sentient hearer? Or with those whose success depends upon large crowds and an immediate favorable response? How must the preacher-prophet conceive of the man to whom he would speak today and whom he would regard as his hearer?

Contemporary literature is replete with works of poetry and prose which give telling and arresting analyses of contemporary man. The preacher-prophet has only to turn to the works of such men as T. S. Eliot, Lewis Mumford, Albert Camus, Martin Heidegger, Jean-Paul Sartre, and Gabriel Marcel to acquaint himself with significant aspects of modern man's life.

He must look beyond modern literature, however, to the Bible itself for his profoundest view of man and his deepest understanding of his hearers today. For it is not in the external character of society (its technological and mechanical achievements, its mass production of commodities and goods) that a correct view of man is to be found but in the essential nature of man himself, in how he reacts to his external environment and in how inwardly hospitable he is to its influences.

While it is true that man's mind and character are shaped by and contain the properties of the things or forces to which it is committed, yet a more important truth is that this commitment is inwardly decided, made, and kept. Thus the material things with which man fills his external environment are themselves morally neutral and cannot reflect more than man's genius and inventive skill. It is man who is moral or immoral. It is he who makes morally neutral things a source of either good or evil. Thus a plethora of modern inventions of themselves could not change the basic view of man as contained in the Bible, although the Bible does not enlarge upon the astounding and monstrous possibilities of man's inventive skill and genius. But it does manifest an understanding of man himself at his deepest and highest spiritual level and at his moral and ethical worst and best.

When the preacher-prophet turns to the Bible for his profoundest understanding of man, he is at the same time turning to the source of his deepest understanding of the man to whom he would speak today as God's spokesman.

III

A third question with which this study will be concerned deals with an inquiry about the preacher-prophet himself: How does the preacher-prophet conceive of his own calling, life, and ministry? Is he to be content with images of himself commonly held by various significant segments of mass society? Are these images immaterial to him? Granted that his own conception of himself and his ministry is of highest moment, how has he arrived at this conception? Is his understanding of himself and his ministry significantly influenced by the society in which he lives and the people whom he expects to be his hearers? If so, in what way or ways are they significantly influenced?

These are not idle, meaningless questions for the preacher-prophet today. He knows, sometimes through a disturbing realization, that he is a product of his times, but that he must be sufficiently emancipated from the life of his day to condemn what is evil in it, to call for a reform of what is bad in it, to encourage the preservation of what is good in it, and to be a pioneer in creating what ought to be characteristic of it. He experiences tensions between the life that is and the life that ought to be, between belonging and not belonging to his times, between his high calling and the faulty ministry he performs, between approval as a workman of God who has no need to be ashamed and a disapproved workman of God who has, nevertheless, won the plaudits of men.

Under the impact of mass society as well as of the resurgent vitalities in the life of the Church, the contemporary preacher-prophet is now being challenged to a more relevant self-portrait. The nature, the claims, and the demands of his calling and ministry are essential matters concerning which he must come to some decision for himself; or they are matters which call for, at the least, a reaffirmation today. The decision must be his, personally arrived at and existentially lived.

IV

Since man in mass society will be discussed in Chapter 2, let us turn now to a consideration of two resurgent vitalities in the life of the Church which are challenging the contemporary preacher-prophet to a more relevant self-portrait.

The resurging importance of preaching today with a corresponding revival of interest in Biblical theology confront the preacher-prophet with a challenge to take a fresh, profound look at himself. For these two developments not only presage a dawning era of great preaching but constitute one of two important factors in the preconditioning of such preaching, the other important factor being the mental and spiritual state of the preacher-prophet himself.

Any era of powerful preaching must be a time in which powerful preachers are produced. The periods of marked decline and decay, and others characterized by powerful and extensive influence in the long history of preaching, were not so much the result of fortuitous happenings as of a spiritual fact always evident in human affairs, namely, that the power of preaching is directly — inevitably and inextricably — related to the preacher of great inward power who himself is molded by internal and external influences of vast consequence. Where there are monsters to be subdued, definite evils to be denounced and attacked, specific forces of moral and spiritual deterioration to be resisted, and particular condemnations of wrongs to be made, the external influences exist to challenge — and to discover! — the man who would speak for God.

Where there is a man who apprehends the spiritual dangers faced by human society as well as by individual persons; who sufficiently comprehends the times to know what the people ought to do; and who, through his inward powers and outward opportunities, his personal convictions of the truth of God in Christ, and the enthralment of a master passion to declare this truth, possesses a sense of his divine call and mission, there are the influences to empower — and to bring forth! — the man who would speak for God.

The contemporary resurgence of the importance of preaching is challenging the preacher-prophet to a new depth of thought about himself as God's spokesman. This new importance which attaches to contemporary preaching is an importance of depth and not one to be interpreted in terms of a widespread attraction to preaching made popular and palatable "with mild heat of holy oratory." It inheres in a profound and Biblical conception of the nature of preaching. The New Testament view of preaching is that it is the proclaiming of the saving deed of God in Christ Jesus (*keryssein*) and the saving deed of God in Christ Jesus proclaimed (*kerygma*).

The place of preaching in the ministry of Jesus has been discussed in a most scholarly way by Robert H. Mounce in chapter 3 of *The Essential Nature of New Testament Preaching*.[1] Theodore Parker Ferris discusses preaching in its relation to the total parish ministry in chapter 1 of his valuable little book *Go Tell the People*.[2] The preacher should read (or reread) these two references with a view to gaining a fresh perspective for the work of the Christian ministry. It is both content and activity.[3] It is that spiritual and miraculous action of God that contemporizes "His historic Self-disclosure" and offers "man the opportunity to respond in faith" each time His Word is truly preached.[4] God becomes a living, present reality *in* the preaching of the Word. They who hear the Word are granted an immediate experience of the creative and redeeming power of God in Christ. This experience is self-authenticating. Nevertheless it is also authenticated by the hearers' conscious relation *in the present* to this same experience which gave birth to and unified the regenerated life of the first believers in Christ in a Christian fellowship, the

[1] Wm. B. Eerdmans Publishing Co., 1960.
[2] Charles Scribner's Sons, 1951.
[3] Mounce, *op. cit.*, p. 153.
[4] *Ibid.*

Church. They who hear the Word possess with conviction the knowledge that God is their God, that He is acting upon *them* and through *them,* and that what He is saying is being said to *them.* They see Him and hear Him and love Him as the God of their personal and present lives. John Knox has written concerning the existential nature of preaching:

> The preacher, as we have so often reminded ourselves, is the preacher of the gospel — the good news of these (ancient) happenings. The Kerugma was at the beginning, as it is still, the proclamation of the life, death, and resurrection of Jesus, of the saving meaning that event proved to have, and of all that is still shaped from it. But it is more than this. Just as preaching does not so much discuss or describe the life of the Christian community as actually to express and convey its concrete meaning, so preaching does more than recount and explain the ancient event. The spirit makes the ancient event in a very real sense an event even now transpiring, and the preaching is a medium of the Spirit's action in doing so. In the preaching, when it is truly itself, the event is continuing or is recurring. God's revealing action in Christ is, still or again, actually taking place.[5]

John Knox is supported in this view of preaching by Robert H. Mounce, who writes:

> True preaching is an event — an event that effectively communicates the power and redemptive activity of God. . . . This, then, is preaching — the timeless link between act and response that prolongs and mediates the redemptive activity of God. Wherever preaching is true to its essential nature, this is what takes place.[6]

Preaching so conceived suggests a more profound conception of the preacher, and gives to Phillips Brooks' definition of preaching as "truth through personality" a deeper relevancy today. How awesome is the thought that the preacher is not only God's spokesman or messenger but the very medium through which God makes His historic Self-disclosure a present event to contemporary man!

The preacher-prophet who accepts this view of the nature of

[5] *The Integrity of Preaching,* Abingdon Press, 1957, p. 92.
[6] *Op. cit.,* p. 155.

preaching as valid and the implied conception of himself as authentic self-knowledge will consider something else in his basic preparation for the preaching ministry, something more important — and ultimate — than the mere acquisition of Biblical and theological knowledge. Biblical and theological knowledge, if pursued diligently and seriously, may make those with the intellectual ability outstanding scholars but not necessarily effective preachers. And effective preachers is what the pulpit — and the congregation — requires and needs. On the other hand, an over-emphasis on the acquisition of knowledge and scholarship may serve to make the more intellectually limited or the mediocre mind (which, incidentally, most of us possess) a self-deprecating preacher who feels that he must depend upon the recitation or reading of the prepared texts of an abler man to be effective as a spokesman for God.

The Church, as the custodian and interpreter of the Christian faith and the trainer of men and women for its various ministries, needs scholars and educators. But it is a mistake, and sometimes a fatal mistake, for the Church to act upon the belief that everyone it trains for the preaching ministry must also be a scholar or an educator. To be sure, the preacher-prophet required by the pulpit and the congregation will always need to be a man who is intellectually competent in his field, with a commanding grasp of general knowledge, but the fact that his mind does not sparkle with brilliance does not preclude his developing a preaching ministry of great perception and power. The pulpit needs preacher-prophets rather than scholars. And it is from the vast multitude of ordinary men that they must come. Yet blessed is the man who has the gifts to become both!

What is more ultimate in the basic preparation of the preacher-prophet is his personal acquaintance and continuing fellowship with Christ, whom his message is about, and his willingness and courage to be used by the Spirit "that the excellency of the power may be of God, and not of us."

The conception of the preacher-prophet suggested by the nature of preaching set forth here also requires that the preacher-prophet consider something else in his basic preparation, more important, and ultimate, than mere correctness of speech and manner achieved through the use of tape recorders and television monitors, which can be equally successful in producing in the talented preacher a reinforced self-satisfaction and in the less gifted the further discomfort of self-consciousness. This would appear to be obvious. Yet it becomes increasingly less obvious to some who are thus involved in the minute achievements of correctness in speech and gesture.

The mechanical and human contrivances employed in pulpit delivery are often apt to become ends in themselves. The preacher-prophet who excels in these things may often, though inadvertently, substitute his own skill and abilities for what should be reserved for the action of the Holy Spirit in the preaching of the Word.

The cultivation of the preacher's every gift and the strengthening of his every weakness is a proper and necessary concern of the preacher-prophet himself and the school in which he is trained. But to grasp the inner meaning of his calling and the gospel he is to proclaim in the fullest possible measure should be of primary importance, and urgency, and should become an increasingly conscious, deliberate, and courageously articulate concern. Browning strikes the balance which is intended in what has been said up to this point:

> For the preacher's merit or demerit,
> It were to be wished that flaws were fewer
> In the earthen vessel, holding treasure,
> But the main thing is, does it hold good measure?
> Heaven soon sets right all other matters![7]

The conception of the preacher-prophet suggested by the nature of preaching set forth here further requires that the man who speaks for God regard himself first and foremost as a preacher, a herald of God. Preaching becomes his primary and central task the same way as it was for the prophets and apostles

[7] "Christmas Eve and Easter Day," Sec. 22, *Complete Poetic and Dramatic Works of Robert Browning*, Houghton Mifflin Co., 1895.

before him. He must not become so enamored of the modern church invention of a multiple ministry that he allows this novel arrangement in some churches today to argue away the preaching ministry being his primary function as a preacher. It would seem rather odd for the man who was sent to speak for God to express a preference for some ministry in the Church other than preaching. To be sure, there will be many functions for the preacher-prophet as a pastor to fulfill besides preaching. But his performance of other duties or a reallocation of responsibilities in the work of the Church should not justify his relinquishment of his historic role while he is in active service. Should he expect anything other than that the preaching of the gospel will remain for him his first love and most inward compulsion?

V

The contemporary revival of interest in Biblical theology also impels the preacher-prophet to a new depth in thinking about himself as the man who speaks for God. For this new interest in Biblical theology involves the correction of a false conception which distinguishes Biblical preaching by an invariable use of a Biblical text and copious quotations from Holy Scripture. Under this false concept more attention is given to the employment (or is the word announcement?) of a text from the Bible and an adroit interspersion of Biblical quotations and references in the sermon than to the actual ideas which are being propounded. Consequently it is quite possible for sermons heavily freighted with Biblical quotations to be quite unbiblical in thought.

Bringing with it a more profound understanding of Biblical preaching today, Biblical theology locates the authenticity of preaching which is truly Biblical in its content. Biblical texts and scriptural references must not be viewed or interpreted as independent or separate passages which can be correctly understood by themselves. They must always be seen and interpreted in relation to their immediate and larger context. The correctness and appropriateness of the interpretation of a particular

Biblical text or passage must be tested by the dominant spirit and central ideas or themes of the Bible. The substance of any sermon which is not consonant with the creative and redemptive significance of the Bible is unbiblical, notwithstanding the employment of a text and the use of copious Biblical quotations and references.

Again, John Knox has written that

biblical preaching is preaching which is centrally concerned with the central biblical event, the event of Christ. The mere treating of incidents in the biblical narrative or scraps of teaching even when done faithfully and in an edifying manner, does not qualify preaching as biblical unless the incidents and teachings are seen and presented in their relation to God's total act of redemption which culminated in the life and death of Jesus, the Resurrection, the coming of the Spirit, and the creation of the church.[8]

The preacher-prophet who accepts the conception of Biblical preaching advanced here must also accept the intellectual demands of this kind of preaching. He must subject himself as an individual and particular preacher to the intellectual processes involved in achieving Biblical comprehension and theological insight. He must recognize this to be a demand which the integrity of preaching makes upon him. He must see superior preparation for his work as a demand which the necessity of his competence as an interpreter of God's Word imposes upon him. He must be faithful and true to the central message of the Bible in every sermon he preaches and assiduously avoid the criticism William Cowper made of a common preaching practice in his day when he wrote:

> How oft, when Paul has served us with a text,
> Has Epictetus, Plato, Tully, preached![9]

Not only must the preacher-prophet be faithful and true to the central truths of the Bible, but he must be faithful and true to his own best abilities and potentialities. He must not be content with

---

[8] *Op. cit.*, p. 20.

[9] "The Time-Piece," *The Task*, Book 2. *A Book of English Literature*, ed. by Franklin Bliss Snyder and Robert Grant Martin, revised by Franklin Bliss Snyder; Macmillan, 1933, p. 804.

imitating, reciting, or reading another preacher's best at the hour appointed for preaching when he is to be the medium through whom God is meant to speak and thus disclose Himself.[10] Rather, he must contribute to the greatness and the power of preaching with the individuality, vigor, and conviction of his own personal effort and inner experience. No man whom God has called to be His spokesman should in faithless effort attempt to substitute what God has done in someone else for an authentic experience of what God could be doing in him. The herald proclaims what has been entrusted to him! The superiority in intellectual quality of the message is not nearly so important as its authenticity and its faithful delivery by the preacher-prophet on whom God can depend. Such a man will have a high estimate of his calling because he maintains a high conception of God who has called him.

In being faithful to God in his calling, the preacher-prophet will be true to himself and faithful to man. And in offering to God his best, the people to whom he speaks will also receive from him his best. For he will give to men what he has received from God. And this will be true of the preacher-prophet, whatever the nature of society and of the generation in which he serves.

---

[10] The preparation of homilies or collections of sermons for the "uninstructed clergy" as an accepted practice appears quite early in the history of preaching. It was a distinctive feature of medieval preaching, and was employed by the English Protestant leaders during the reign of Queen Elizabeth (1558-1603) to instruct, upgrade and guide the "less cultured preachers" of English Protestantism.

The use of homilies was both helpful and harmful. It provided needed sermonic and parish helps to the clergy, most of whom were quite limited in ability. But it also fostered a dependence upon such assistance, many times at the cost of individual initiative and disciplined study, originality and personal spiritual force. Moreover, a limited clergy, that chose to commit to memory the prepared homilies and recite them or even to read them outright, brought no little disrespect to the clergy in general.

Opinion may differ widely with regard to the extent to and the manner in which books of sermons should be employed by the clergy today. But there should be no room for difference of opinion over whether we should, in every case, do what will bring respect and dignity to our calling (and profession in contemporary life) and honor to Him who has sent us.

CHAPTER TWO

A Man Sent from God

From earliest times, God has chosen to speak to the world through men. No other instrumentality could have served this purpose so well, for it is His character and will that He has purposed that the world should know. Being a Person, He needed personality through which to give a full revelation of Himself. Thus He chose men. He spoke His word and revealed Himself in Old Testament times through the personalities of imperfect men — men whose receptivity was conditioned by their capacity. His perfect Word could only be communicated by His will perfectly revealed through perfect personality. Christ alone had perfect insight into the nature and will of the Father. Through Him is perfectly revealed to us today the mission and message of men who would be God's messengers. Since we cannot expect a greater than Christ to come into the world to reveal God more perfectly than He did while in the flesh, the contemporary preacher-prophet's task and mission now is that of bearing witness to all men that Christ Jesus is the saving deed of God.

But to bear witness means more than simply to *tell* "the old, old story" of the life, death, and resurrection of our Lord and Saviour Jesus Christ. To bear witness today as the herald of Christ, the preacher-prophet must so offer himself for the preaching of the gospel that the historic content and experience of the *kerygma* (the message proclaimed) is received and witnessed as an event instantaneously occurring — and recurring — in the act of preaching through him and in the presence of all who have eyes to see and ears to hear and hearts to receive. As God disclosed Himself in His Word uttered by the prophets and apostles, and pre-eminently in Jesus Christ, so God in Christ will reveal Himself to men today through His Word proclaimed by the heralds whom He has sent.

I

The preacher-prophet must possess the conviction that, as a spokesman for God in Christ, through whom He is reconciling the world unto Himself, he is a divinely used human instrumentality. He is an instrumentality chosen for the unfolding and realization of the will of God in the world through Christ Jesus. He is in the world as one who has been sent and who has for proclamation a message he has been given. This was God's revelation to the author of the Fourth Gospel concerning John the Baptist:

> There was a man sent from God, whose name was John. The same came for a witness, to bear witness of the Light, that all men through him might believe. He was not that Light, but *was sent* to bear witness to that Light (John 1:9).

This is no less God's revelation to the preacher-prophet today concerning himself. God who reveals to the preacher-prophet the authenticity of his calling also proves the authenticity of his proclamation by the miracle it performs during every act of true preaching. His voice is heard above the ancient printed Word as it comes to the hearer through the medium of the human voice and the preacher-prophet's personality. His Word has a contemporaneous note and a deeply personal appeal. The hearer knows that this is God's Word of old and yet it comes to him as a new and timely message. What is proclaimed to the group is heard simultaneously by the individual. What is spoken as one general message is heard as various specific messages. The language of God's Word in preaching has a common translator in the Holy Spirit.

When God speaks to us through the preached Word, we do not hear His message to another age, to another people — we hear a message addressed directly to us. When through the preaching of the Word we hear Amos pleading for justice and righteousness at Bethel, we are aware of the pleadings of a living Voice constraining us to do justice and righteousness. We hear the Master's call to follow Him when He bids His first disciples to leave their nets and become fishers of men. And we who are repentant know that our sins are forgiven and we have received assurance of pardon when He remits the sins of a lame man on the Sabbath day. The "healing of His seamless dress" brings healing to us as virtue goes out of His garment to heal a distressed woman of her affliction. And we are comforted in bereavement and loss when He says to Martha and Mary: "I am the resurrection, and the life" (John 11:25). This is indeed the miracle of preaching: a revelation of God is mediated to us through the preaching of the Word.

To those who can *hear,* this revealed Word is more than the revelation *contained* in the Bible. It is a fresh, timely, but eternal revelation mediated to us *through* the preaching of the written Word. Such a miracle could be performed only through the medium of a man *sent* from God, the authenticity of whose preaching is attested by the miracle itself.

But true preaching may have a directly opposite effect upon other hearers. Preaching to them may not be wisdom at all, but foolishness. They may hear no word to which they should cling more than to another. They may see no act to which they should attach the wonder of a miracle. The preaching of the Word may not draw but repel them; it may not energize but enervate them. It may bring no healing of mind or comfort of spirit, no visions grand or purposes noble, no living word or real presence. The power in preaching may simply not exist for them.

Indeed, the power of preaching cannot be known except to him who is *ready* to hear and *willing* to receive the self-revelations of God made manifest through preaching. Men cannot hear without a preacher but even with a preacher they cannot hear until they want to hear.

This is why the preacher-prophet must be incessant in preaching the gospel. This is why he must be "instant in season, out of season." Men will not always willingly hear or endure the whole truth of God simply and unadornedly proclaimed. With "itching ears" they will insist upon novelty, variety, eloquence. They will prefer to hear the topics of the day or some fascinatingly strange subject interestingly presented and cleverly discussed. Thus a demonstration of the Spirit and power during the act of preaching will not be witnessed or experienced by some because they have already developed a preference for the sensational and clever word of man rather than the reproving, comforting, simple and redemptive Word of God in Christ Jesus.

The Word, however, must be preached incessantly against the possibility, on the one hand, that man may become ready to hear and receive it at any moment and, on the other, that the preacher-prophet may give "full proof" of his ministry "with all long-suffering and doctrine," being fully conscious of his utter dependence upon the God who sends him. Without God's Spirit, he is powerless. Without His commission, he is without a message.

II

The man sent from God is not only a divinely used instrumentality, but a messenger who declares God's truth under the constraint of an inescapable sense of mission. His mission is one from which he cannot release himself. If he could, he most certainly should. He knows that any calling that can be regarded lightly and served at will is no calling at all; that when God lays a constraint upon the preacher-prophet's heart, he cannot for long resist it. "Woe is unto me," declared the Apostle Paul, "if I preach not the gospel!" (I Cor. 9:16). These are not the words of a man who of himself has chosen to preach. They are rather the words of a man who knew that he had been chosen and, therefore, *must* preach. God had hidden His Word in Paul's heart, and had placed His seal thereon. In making Paul the obedient servant of a "heavenly vision," He made him a slave of the gospel. This man was thus fortified to endure without end the "slings and arrows of outrageous fortune" and with unabating ardour, to "press on toward the goal unto the prize of the high calling of God in Christ Jesus" (Phil. 3:14); he could live independent of circumstance, knowing both how to be abased and how to abound — all because he was strengthened by Christ in the mission for which he had been chosen of God.

God always chooses the man who himself is ultimately willing to choose to be chosen. In such a man is the predisposition of the preacher-prophet, albeit often long unknown or undesired. But this is the man whom God at last seizes to be His spokesman — the man who is peculiarly prepared by temperament, mind, and spirit to be His voice. Moreover, God has confronted only that man with the crucial issues of the moment who himself has recognized these issues and is zealous for their resolution. And God has led only that man who is hopefully impatient with the sins and errors of the times into a discovery of the truths which, if applied, will abolish them.

Amos was neither a prophet nor a prophet's son when he observed with intense indignation the injustice and wickedness of Bethel. Those who could recognize the injustice and wickedness of this place would hardly expect an Amos to cry out with the deepest impatience against "the king's sanctuary and court." He belonged neither to the official priesthood nor to the recognized prophetic order. He was only a herdsman and a gatherer of wild figs. Yet, in the sight of Jehovah, he was the man to speak. He had lived close enough to Jehovah and far enough away from the sins of Bethel to be Jehovah's spokesman. And he was chosen to speak.

The moment and the occasion demanded just such a man as Amos. He felt compelled to speak. He was willing to speak. And he spoke, not in his name but in the name of the Lord — he spoke *for* the Lord. Amos had a profound and clear comprehension of the situation in which he found himself. His mission was clear. He could not escape it; nor did he wish to; for he and Jehovah had reached an agreement with each other.

John the Baptist, too, could no more resist standing on the banks of Jordan and over against Jerusalem crying, "Repent ye: for the kingdom of heaven is at hand" (Matt. 3:2) than he could resist being himself. For he and his mission were one. He had incorporated into his own personality the message which he now propounded. He was a man sent from God for just this time and occasion. God had chosen him. He had sided with God. He had accepted his commission.

The man of God who is possessed of a sense of mission — a sense of the work to which he has been called — is also cognizant of and zealous for his ambassadorship. He knows that his life and work are to be representative of the God who has sent him forth. He is obliged to represent *one* God, *one* country, and to speak *one* language. Like John the Baptist, he is a forerunner of the Christ of faith. It is his responsibility to make the hilly ways level and the crooked paths straight for the coming of Christ into the life of today. This man of God is to do this by being a witness of Christ as the saving deed of God, the true Light whose light the preacher-prophet himself reflects. For men whose visions have but a short range must see Christ through him. Those whose faith cannot reach beyond the realm of the senses must believe in his belief. If the preacher-prophet fails to proclaim the gospel, the people cannot hear. If he fails to reflect the true Light in his own life, many will not see. Without the sent preacher-prophet, men will not know the redemptive power of God's Word. So it is of the greatest moment that the man who declares God's Word to men does so out of the deepest consciousness of his ambassadorship.

Moreover, this man must represent one realm — the city of God. His highest obedience and loyalty must be to that "better *country*, that is, an heavenly [realm]" (Heb. 11:10). And he must live *now* as though he already possesses it. As it was for Abraham, God's tents must be his home until he has found the "city which hath foundations, whose builder and maker *is* God" (Heb. 11:10).

Too often we confuse good earthly forms of government and structures of society with the reign of God and His Kingdom on earth. But there is no form of government, however good, and no structure of society, however fructifying, that can be equated with the Kingdom of God. God's Kingdom is other than man's highest achievements, although God works through human endeavor. The Kingdom is an act and a gift of God to those who live in this world in the consciousness that God is the ultimate reference to their life. It is the Divine working through and above human instrumentality, winning men now to citizenship in the realm of the Spirit. God's Kingdom on earth is a realm where His will reigns as the will of men.[1]

This is the Kingdom to which the man sent from God belongs. And as a citizen of this divine realm, he speaks a divine language. While all members of the Kingdom of God speak this divine language, it is pre-eminently the language of that man who is God's special spokesman — the man who declares the eternal Word of truth. It is necessary, therefore, that the preacher-prophet live in the consciousness of this fact. For he must not confuse his word with the Word of God. Moreover, he is not to feel that he is obligated to make immediate pronouncements upon every current event. He is to wait until God is ready to speak through him. He must somehow know when God is ready to speak and what it is the Lord God would have him say to His people. Otherwise he will be guilty of presenting his own words as the Word of God, and of speaking on superficial, transitory concerns of the day; or he will find himself addressing his words only to the manifestations of the real and deeper issues of the times rather than being the medium through which God gives light and pronounces judgment upon the central and crucial issues of life. Only what God says through the preacher-prophet is of

[1] This is not to suggest, however, that we as Christians should not work in this world to achieve the best society, making it as Christian as possible. We must not commit the error of equating our best possible historical achievements with what is achievable beyond history. Moreover, we must not be ensnared by human pride in believing that what is achievable in the realm of the Spirit can be realized with material means. For a stimulating and realistic discussion of a Christian society, see T. S. Eliot, *Christianity and Culture,* and *The Idea of a Christian Society,* Harcourt, Brace and Company, 1949; and *What the Christian Hopes for in Society,* Wayne H. Cowan, ed., Association Press, 1957.

enduring pertinence. Whatever the preacher-prophet says without a revelation of God, regardless of how well he says it, is spoken to the wind. He is sent from God to speak a divine language; no other language becomes him.

III

When God lays His constraint upon a man and sends him forth amongst men who are hostile or indifferent to His will for the world, He does not send him forth unequal to the demands that will be made upon him. He makes his feet "like hinds' feet," and gives him shoes of "iron and brass." In other words, He makes him equal to every climb, to every leap and precipice. This man sent from God is made equal to every sudden and unusual demand made upon him in the fulfillment of his mission. God empowers each of His chosen with an abundance of interior resources which he is expected to appropriate and replenish. God aligns him on the side of forces in this world which are superior to those of destruction.

Leadership in the cause of God implies a superior equipment for living and a life above the average. He who would "sweat" so much for the world must first of all "sweat" some for himself until the stream of history is purified within his own soul. Only then will he have in his possession something superior to give, something worth witnessing about — a possession which alone can justify his claim to leadership. When Lawrence of England sought to become the leader of the tribes of Arabia, he was told this by their leaders: "You must eat the same food that we eat, find shelter in the same tents in which we dwell, accept the same risks that we accept, meet the same difficulties we meet, live the same life we live — and live it better than we do." This was the requirement placed upon Lawrence for leadership.

No less a requirement is imposed upon the preacher-prophet today who would be a leader in the cause of Christianity. He can accept and meet this requirement only as he allows God to empower him with an abundance of superior interior resources. Only if he is empowered by God who sent him can he remain true to his high calling when others fall prey to "the fell clutch of circumstance."

There is in the man sent from God and thus empowered for leadership a divine process at work which men about him can neither see nor know. They only know that he is triumphant in his faith and courage, that he is expendable; that he possesses unfailing power. But to know even this is to marvel at it, for only one who has experienced it can know the secret of such victorious living. That man alone can conceive of the marvelous things that God can do with and for one who utterly depends upon Him. There is between God and His chosen a marvelous secret — God's process of inner filling known only to Him and the one whom He fills. The following old madrigal admirably expresses this thought:

> As torrents in summer
> Half-dried in their channels
> Suddenly rise, though the
> Sky is still cloudless,
> For rain has been falling
> Far off at their fountains;
>
> So hearts that are fainting
> Grow full to o'erflowing,
> And they that behold it
> Marvel, and know not
> That God at their fountains
> Far off has been raining![2]

A parallel may be drawn (if not pushed too far) between the empowered preacher-prophet and the Nile river in its passing through nearly two thousand miles of sandy expanse without rain or tributary. In this desert land, Egypt is dependent for its fertility, for its very life, upon the Nile. Summer comes, and the river battles against the desert and the sun without any visible help. Yet while all other rivers are receding and drying up, the great Nile overflows its banks to render a much needed service to this land.

---

[2] Longfellow's *Tales of a Wayside Inn*, "The Musician's Tale," Sect. 12, entitled, "The Noon of Nidoras," stanzas 7, 8.

The secret of this overflowing is to be found up in the Abyssinian mountains. There rain falls at the very source of the Blue Nile, giving it an indispensable resource for its greatest struggle: to bid defiance to the infinite sand and "to fertilize the desert a thousand miles away."[3] They who marvel at its overflowing its banks when all other rivers are receding may not know that at its source the rain has been falling. So it is with the man sent from God. Men marvel at his ability to meet the sudden and unusual demands that others cannot meet. They marvel at his victorious vitality, for they know not that God at the fountain of his life "far off has been raining."

The empowered and triumphant lives of men divinely chosen and sent in other times to be witnesses of the true Light, which is Christ, are God's revelation to those of us who would be His messengers today. Through these empowered and sustained lives, He speaks directly to us. He speaks to us of our high potentiality as men sent from God. He speaks to us of our mission and our destiny as preacher-prophets. He speaks to us of the inescapable constraint which He has laid upon us, and of the unfailing resources of His power. And He speaks to us of Christ Jesus with whom we company here in the Spirit as truly as the disciples did in the flesh. Through these lives, and pre-eminently through the life of Christ, we catch new glimpses of God's truth, and are compelled to pray with Frances R. Havergal:

> Lord, speak to me, that I may speak
> In living echoes of Thy tone;
> As Thou hast sought, so let me seek,
> Thy erring children lost and lone.
>
> O teach me, Lord, that I may teach
> The precious things Thou dost impart;
> And wing my words, that they may reach
> The hidden depths of many a heart.
>
> O lead me, Lord, that I may lead
> The wandering and the wavering feet;
> O feed me, Lord, that I may feed
> The hungering ones with manna sweet.

[3] Emil Ludwig, *The Nile*, Viking Press, 1938, p. 101.

> O strengthen me, that while I stand
> Firm on the Rock, and strong in Thee,
> I may stretch out a loving hand
> To wrestlers with the troubled sea.
>
> O fill me with Thy fullness, Lord,
> Until my very heart o'erflow
> In kindling tho't and glowing word,
> Thy love to tell, Thy praise to show.
>
> O use me, Lord, use even me,
> Just as Thou wilt, and when, and where;
> Until Thy blessed face I see,
> Thy rest, Thy joy, Thy glory share.[4]

IV

At least two final words are necessary before this chapter is concluded. The first is that the writer has not meant to give the impression here that the preacher-prophet is a superman or belongs to some order of beings a little higher than the angels. Yet he would maintain that the man sent from God is specially endowed and specially gifted. His conscious possession of a message from God and the ability effectively to proclaim it would make this so. But his endowment and gifts are not his sole properties. These things are given within the context of his limitations and liabilities as a human being as well as that of his possibilities and strengths. In other words, the preacher-prophet suffers the frailties and weaknesses of the flesh as do other men. Paul says that he is an earthen vessel which gains its importance by what it holds. And because of what it contains, it is compelled to be careful with itself.

One would fail to comprehend a great truth about the preacher-prophet were one only to recognize that this man possesses weaknesses and frailties. The important truth is not that he has these liabilities, for these are common to all men, but that they serve a peculiar function in him. Furthermore, these liabilities are not present in the man sent from God in order that they may serve a special function in him; rather, they are made to serve

[4] *Mennonite Hymnary*, No. 296, Mennonite Book Concern, 1940.

this special function in him because they are there. Then, more explicitly, weaknesses and infirmities may become sources of strength and power to the preacher-prophet. Because he knows they are there within him, he is impelled to act in a way as though they were not there, gaining strength and power through a conscious effort either to transcend or to transform them. He becomes like the tortoise in the race with the hare. The tortoise which, by nature, is slow, dares not stop for a moment in his race with the hare because of this liability. But the hare which, by nature, is fast does not feel any compulsion to keep running until the race is won. His strength in being fast allows him to *linger* in the race. And he loses the race to the tortoise. His very strength proved to be his greatest liability.

To be sure, a source of the preacher-prophet's strength and power is to be found in an unknown degree in the very centers of his weakness, his frailty, his peculiarities, even his remembrance of guilt of some personal sin long forgiven. Paul was continually pressed on by his "heavenly vision," but it was more than this vision which motivated him. He never forgot that he had been a persecutor of the Church. He remembered his past and must as often have felt a prick of conscience because of what he had done. He wrote to the Corinthian Church:

> For I am the least of the apostles, that am not meet to be called an apostle, because I persecuted the church of God. But by the grace of God I am what I am: and his grace which was bestowed upon me was not in vain; but I laboured more abundantly than they all: yet not I but the grace of God which was with me (I Cor. 15:9,10).

Remembering his physical weakness and frail appearance, he wrote further to the Corinthian Church:

> And was with you in weakness, and in fear, and in much trembling. And my speech and my preaching was not with enticing words of man's wisdom, but in demonstration of the Spirit and of power: That your faith should not stand in the wisdom of men, but in the power of God (I Cor. 2:3-5).

To affirm one's weakness can mean to overcome it if by this affirmation one, by God's grace, is renouncing it.

Certainly Peter was made bold to preach the gospel and, with John, to defy the Jewish council not only because he had received the Holy Ghost but because he remembered his guilt in denying his Master and forsaking Him during those fateful days of the Passion and Crucifixion. The force and fearlessness of his words before the council would suggest that this is true:

> For we cannot but speak the things which we have seen and heard (Acts 4:20).

What a blessing — this chance to make up for his former failure to speak up for his Lord and Master!

The preacher-prophet is an earthen vessel. His limitations and liabilities may be many in some cases, and few but great in others. Yet God chooses him and not someone else!

A second final word is this. The writer has meant to give the impression that the preacher-prophet can be a power for God and an exemplar of an extraordinary spiritual life by the action of God's grace within him. God demonstrates what He can do with "frail creatures of dust." Again listen to Paul's recounting his plea to God to take away the thorn in his flesh:

> And he said unto me, My grace is sufficient for thee: for my strength is made perfect in weakness. Most gladly therefore will I rather glory in my infirmities, that the power of Christ may rest upon me. Therefore I take pleasure in infirmities, in reproaches, in necessities, in persecutions, in distresses for Christ's sake: for when I am weak, then am I strong (II Cor. 12:9-10).

But the preacher-prophet does not enjoy this spiritual boon or possess great spiritual power unconditionally. His calling and inward strength are morally and spiritually conditioned. He, like other men, can suffer alienation from God by willful disobedience. And this separation must of necessity and evitably bring with it all of the spiritual darkness, impoverishment, emptiness, and anguish which it brings to any man who falls away from God and His way. But the preacher-prophet's moral and spiritual failure is no simple failure, like other men's. In the eyes of other men, he has betrayed not only his God and himself, but them as well. For even recalcitrant, sinful men there must be examples of the life they know they ought to live but are not willing to live just yet. There must be visible proofs that God is holy and just and unfailing in His power since they will not permit these things to be true just yet in them. The life they should live men wish to see in their leaders, whether they hear and follow them or not!

Be this as it may, the preacher-prophet is subject, nevertheless, to the withdrawal of God's Spirit and power when his heart is no longer hospitable to the Spirit's company. He may continue to do the work of the preacher-prophet but God will not be with him. This withdrawal does not ultimately hurt God's Word. It is never in danger of losing its efficacy because of the moral turpitude or spiritual laxity of God's spokesman. But the preacher-prophet himself is in danger of being lost. Paul recognized this fact when he wrote to the Corinthian Church:

> I therefore so run, not as uncertainly; so fight I, not as one that beateth the air: but I keep under my body, and bring it into subjection: lest that by any means, when I have preached to others, I myself should be a castaway (I Cor. 9:26-27).

The true preacher-prophet will not hazard the Word of God in Christ nor place in jeopardy his own soul by willful disobedience to the God who called him. Rather, he will live in the freedom of singlemindedness under the God to whom he is committed. He will nourish the inward satisfaction of a message faithfully proclaimed. He will desire the strength and power of an integrity maintained in the mission on which he has been sent. God will be the power channeled through him, and he will keep himself an offering "fit for the Master's use."

What God says to proclaim, this he will proclaim. Where God tells him to go, this is where he will go. What God bids him to do, this is what he will do. For this end was he sent into the world. And he is ultimately content to pursue it to the end of his service here.

CHAPTER THREE

Communicating with Mass Man

The gravest error the preacher-prophet can make today in preaching the "good news" of God is to assume that his proclamation is being heard in an atmosphere of Christian understanding and that what he is saying is accepted by his hearers as good news. For today the opposite of this is largely true. Most people embrace a religious ethos and would be loathe to discard all religious forms for no religious forms at all, but this ethos finds its meaning in a frame of reference quite different from the one in which the forms of our traditional Christian beliefs and doctrines are set.

This situation is a troublesome one for the preacher-prophet and confronts him with a problem of communication. And he must understand that at least a part of the solution of the problem is to be found in how modern man and his society got the way they are. Even this would not actually be contributing to the solution of the problem; it would merely be contributing to our preparation for solving the problem of communicating the gospel to mass man.

I

The problem of communicating the gospel today cannot be quickly solved because it has not been quickly created. Its history reaches back half a millennium; it is co-extensive with the rise and spread of our civilization, which brought with it the secularization of life and the severance of civilized people from their cultural moorings.

Although the civilizing process begins at different times and at different rates of speed in different primitive societies, the civilization which marked the beginning of the modern period in the world, produced modern man and eventuated in mass society, dates back to the fourteenth and fifteenth centuries. The climate and soil for the secularization of life were produced by the Renaissance and the Reformation. The seed was actually planted by the Enlightenment, or Rationalism. It was nurtured by Romanticism. And its growth was accelerated by the rise and rapid territorial spread of trade and commerce and the phenomenal development of industry and technology. These are the source and substance of our civilization but at the same time resistants to and operants against culture as understood in its more primitive and fundamental sense.[1]

It is necessary here to state the distinction between culture and civilization which is accepted and held valid in these pages. Certainly it is important — and necessary — to contrast the two in order clearly to understand modern man's problem as a hearer of the Word and the preacher-prophet's problem of communicat-

[1] On its cultural and spiritual side, aspects of the subject with which we are mostly concerned here, the secularization of life in the West stems from the very complex forces which operated to liberate man from the classical Biblical world view and its predominating influence upon Western society. This world view was reflected and advocated by, insisted upon, and vigorously maintained by, the cultural and religious authorities up to the Renaissance. But with the "breakthrough" of new knowledge under the impulse of an adventurous and scientific spirit and a new valuation of man himself as a worthful, inquisitive, thinking, feeling, and autonomous being came medieval man's revolt. He revolted against the static pattern of life in the limited world to which he belonged as well as against his cultural and religious traditions, institutions, and authorities.

In revolting against the fixed and limited life of the West, medieval man not only passed from a finite into an infinite world, but he surrendered in this transition the traditional absolutes, loyalties, and norms of judgment according to which he had made his choices, established his values, arrived at his certainties, and sensed his spiritual security.

The humanistic, rationalistic, and idealistic forces which operated to liberate medieval man from old cultural and religious tyrannies and present him with possibilities of a new freedom or enslavement created the periods and movements which we know as the Renaissance, the Reformation, Rationalism, and Romanticism.

ing the Word to modern man. At least with the distinction between culture and civilization the social scientist can be of help to us.

Coming from the pen of one who, as a professor of sociology at the University of Chicago and later at Fisk University, had trained a whole generation of sociologists, is the following useful contrast between culture and civilization in his posthumous work *Race and Culture*:

> Culture is the sort of order existing in a society which has a cult or a religion. It preserves morale and enables the group to act collectively.... If we could use the word *culture* to refer to a society that has a moral order and *civilization* to refer to the order that applies to a territorial group, we could bring out the important distinction more clearly. What we call civilization is always a territorial affair. It comes about by trade and commerce. We cannot be satisfied with a mere recognition that there are cultural areas, as the anthropologists have used that term. Civilization is built up by the absorption of foreign ethnic groups, by undermining them, and by secularizing their cult and sacred order....
>
> What actually happens is that the smaller ethnic groups become secularized and break down. Civilization is fundamentally a territorial affair. It undermines the smaller cultures and by secularizing them furnishes release to the individual from the controls to which he is accustomed.[2]

A much earlier sociologist of distinction contrasted culture and civilization in terms of *Gemeinschaft* and *Gesellschaft*, the sacred and secular societies.[3] He pointed out that the *Gemeinschaft* is the small, organic society characterized by immobility, familial, neighborly and sacral relationships. The *Gesellschaft* is a more complex and flexible society characterized by mobility, loose associations, efficiency, temporal attitudes, and commercial relationships. Its means and methods of social control are not filial piety, custom, and respect for tradition as in the *Gemeinschaft*, but rather what is fashionable as public opinion, and common, acceptable practice in conduct.

[2] Robert Ezra Park, *The Free Press*, 1950, p. 16 (posthumously published).

[3] Ferdinand J. Tonnies, *Gemeinschaft und Gesellschaft*, 1897.

The distinctions between culture and civilization pointed out by the two distinguished authors cited here are informative. On the basis of these distinctions it may be submitted that in a culture, as the term is used here, religion is an indispensable integrant of group and personal life; the cult is primary and serves as the anchor and control of the group. The individual is sure of his standing in the group and knows what the group demands of him. His whole society is characterized by a "fundamental conformity," to use J. H. Oldham's phrase; it is motivated by a common religious ethos. Consequently, secured by the cultural moorings of the group to which he belongs, the individual's life is secure; it has meaning, purpose, and support. He does not experience the internal contradictions and insecurities known by the individual whose culture or cult life has been "undermined" by civilization (as the term is here used).

Civilization, which tends to secularize life by breaking down the moral order and discrediting the basic assumptions by which a people have lived and to which they have grown accustomed, leaves the individual and his society, at least for a time, in a state of disintegration. It releases man from a moral order and a system of religious worship or ritual which may be too restrictive and binding for his advancement, but it does not immediately offer him something that can take the place of that from which he has been released. This situation man, in time, may be able to remedy for himself. But in the meantime the civilization he has won (or the civilization which has captured him) has produced a disintegrated society.

The triumph of civilization over culture for the possession of man has resulted in a contemporary society which is at the same time mechanically efficient and spiritually uninformed, materially affluent and morally impoverished, intellectually capable but anarchical in values. There is no fundamental conformity of Christian assumptions, attitudes and values to provide modern man with adequate social controls and to preserve contemporary society itself from its many internal contradictions. Civilization has no cult through which man may be related meaningfully and spiritually to the realities of his existence now and in the future, although it is possible for modern man to develop one for himself in time.

This all means that there can be no adequate communication and understanding between the preacher-prophet and modern man, his hearer, unless and until there are commonly acknowledged Christian assumptions, attitudes, and values serving as the frame of reference within which the proclamation of the Gospel is heard *as it is proclaimed*. It is quite possible in a society such as ours which is characterized by an "anarchy of values," "the loss of criteria," and "the loss of ritual" for hearers of the Word to miss the main import of the gospel message even though it has been proclaimed in purity and with power. The one who proclaims the gospel and the one to whom the gospel is proclaimed must meet for communication and understanding on at least the common ground of word meanings and their connotations and a religious ethos set in the same frame of reference. But even this, it will be found, is not sufficient to establish real communication with the modern hearer of the Word. The real problem may lie elsewhere.

And quite often it does. As confused and disintegrated as contemporary life appears to be, most people are not so lost in their alienation from organized Christianity that they are ready to throw overboard the only forms of Christian belief and practice they have known, and perhaps one time experienced, simply because they no longer find the religious experience of organized church life satisfactory to them. Many today do hear the voice of the Son of God through His servants of the Word, although it is "faint-voiced through long silence." Many are attempting to find the real convictions of the Christian faith in other pursuits and collectivities than the fellowship of the Church and its program of life and work.

II

But why look for the real convictions of the Christian faith elsewhere than in the Church which is the custodian of this faith and the place where this faith is proclaimed from Sunday to Sunday?

Many will answer in the first place that what the Church has to say through its preacher-prophets is irrelevant to the main and pressing concerns of our mass-produced contemporary life. The chief concern of mass society is man himself. He is concerned about his own historical existence and is in need of a real meaning for his life today, here and now. But he feels, whether rightly or wrongly, that too long and too frequently has the Church emphasized man's relation to the world to come and has offered little help in his struggle for a this-worldly mode and meaning of existence.

Not all modern men would dispense with God for the sake of their own enthronement. This is not the kind of anthropocentric concern which preoccupies many. They would find more relevant to their present pressing need a presentation — even exaltation — of God in terms of His relation and meaning to man in man's historical existence, in the claims and demands that his this-worldly relationships make upon him!

Before the existential character of modern man's daily life was forced into his consciousness, a sermon on the doctrine of God which emphasized His attributes of omnipotence, omniscience and omnipresence may have been a pleasant mental excursion on a Sunday morning. But today God must be preached in the light of man's life and death options. God as a tenet of faith must become a subject of existential concern to man for whom the world in which his historical existence is spent was created. Thus any preaching which is not anthropocentric in the sense that it reflects the special and central position of man in the world as presented in the Biblical view of "Man in the Cosmos"[4] and God's solicitations on his behalf for his life here and now is not only irrelevant but unbiblical.

If preaching is to be Biblical preaching, at least in one sense,

---

[4] Emil Brunner, *Man in Revolt*, Westminster Press, 1947, chapter 18.

it must emphasize without apology and misgivings the anthropocentric view of the Bible. About this view Brunner says:

> Man is not a bit of the world; he stands over against all creaturely
> existence as something special, as a new dimension. It is not due
> to naïveté, but is the necessary consequence of the Biblical idea
> of God that the Biblical picture of the world is absolutely
> anthropocentric, to such an extent indeed that in the Bible the
> world and man are frequently interchangeable ideas. The world of
> which the Bible speaks is always the world for man, the world in
> which the fate of man is of supreme importance. Man is in the
> centre of the world, in spite of the fact that God is His Creator
> and Lord, as He is the Creator and Lord of the world. God has
> placed man as lord over the creatures, He has ordered the world
> for him.[5]

Lest the impression be given that Brunner's statement quoted
here is one-sided in emphasis, another passage must be cited
from this same work. Brunner adds this further point:

> The distinctive element in the Biblical idea of the world is this,
> that man, for whom the world is ordered as its summit, goal, and
> its end, is also himself God's creature, servant and not master;
> one who receives and not one who sends; a reflection, not an
> original light; a dependent and not an independent being. It is
> the creaturely being, man, who has been created out of nothing,
> who is not eternal, not unconditioned, who is wholly dependent,
> whom God makes lord over His creation. Man is master of the
> world because and in so far as God makes him so, because through
> the fact that God creates him only in His image, He allows him to
> have the privilege of being subject and being spirit, of freedom and
> of creative activity, and endows him with those powers by means of
> which man can actually "make subject unto him" "that which is
> under him."[6]

If the preacher-prophet accepts this as the Biblical view of
man in the world, then he must be willing to accept man's
legitimate preoccupation with life in this world as a vital, and
Christian, concern to which he, as preacher-prophet, must bring
the light of the gospel. It is no wonder that modern man dis-
misses much of the contemporary preaching he hears as irrelevant,

[5] *Ibid.*, p. 409.
[6] *Ibid.*, p. 410.

although it reflects what the preacher-prophet knows to be Christian ideas. The trouble often is that too much contemporary preaching starts at the wrong point of emphasis of the problems and issues with which mass man is confronted. This would be largely corrected by a more this-worldly emphasis in today's preaching and the sacramentalization of the natural and normal processes of man's daily life and work. God must be verified for modern man not only in the historical events upon which the preaching of the preacher-prophet is based but in these natural and normal processes of man's life and work.

The preacher-prophet must lead modern man to find the meaning of his existence and his approaches to God *in* the economic, social and political arrangements of mass society and *through* whatever intellectual and moral competence he now possesses. It is simply not enough for mass man to have pointed out to him the inadequacies and perils of his spiritual experience, of the mass-produced substitutes for his own direct personal and spiritual experience, of his intellectual and moral relativism, and of the secular nature of the society to which he belongs. Modern man is not unaware of his predicament. His problem is to discover what he can do about it. But the absolute terms in which directions are laid out for him by the Church and much of the preaching he hears complicates rather than simplifies his problem. This leads us to a second reason why many persons today have turned away from the Church to search for the real convictions of the Christian faith elsewhere.

III

Modern man finds such a disparity between what is preached to him as the Christian faith and what is possible in the present set of circumstances under which he lives in mass society that he tacitly, if not unblushingly, ignores what the preacher-prophet says. Hence there is erected another block to an effectual communication of the gospel to him.

The contemporary world of man has many areas which are not black or white but grey. Man faces the necessity of making moral decisions and choices in these areas of human and daily activity. But because of the nature of the situation itself in these areas, his decisions frequently are at best only morally relative. He faces not only the dilemma but the forced option of choosing between two evils or two really undesirable alternatives. Must he refuse to make a decision because there is no ideal choice for him to make? Or can he expect the understanding and judgment of the Church that he is serving the will of God when he chooses the lesser of two evils or undesirable alternatives?

Should he, for example, support engagement in limited warfare in preference to unlimited warfare when one or the other is the only course open to his nation or the United Nations? Should he support the use of the national guard to enforce a U.S. Supreme Court decision on desegregation of schools in one of the southern states in preference to supporting a state's open defiance of this decision and its resistance to it? Should he insist upon the protection of a corrupt and arrogant labor leader in the absence of sufficient legal grounds to incarcerate him in preference to the employment of unconstitutional, illegal or even extra-legal means to depose him? Should he endorse and make use of artificial insemination as a means of bringing children into his home in preference to ignoring the serious threat that childless marriages pose for some couples? And should he work in the factory on Sundays as well as other days of the week in compliance with management's work schedule in preference to risking the loss of his job by refusing to do so?

Multitudinous and omnipresent are the moral decisions modern man must make in the grey areas of contemporary life. But the preacher-prophet who insists upon black-and-white decisions in such areas of man's activity, simply because it is his business to hold forth ideal and Christian ends for man's life and work, is sure to alienate many of his hearers because they can expect no support or guidance from him in what they know to be not the most ideal moral solution to many of their problems but the only solutions possible under the circumstances. What they find morally possible in many situations of their daily existence may be widely divergent from the Christian ideals proclaimed from the pulpit. Thus again the lines of communication between them and the gospel proclaimed to them by the preacher-prophet are severed.

The preacher-prophet can mend these lines by facing the realities in the moral situations confronted by mass man and helping him to discover the will of God for his life and work through the only real experiences he can have and through the only moral choices he can make *at the time*.

The following comment to the Christian man is instructive to the preacher-prophet:

> Moral choices are not made in a vacuum. Good motives and 'goodwill' are not enough; we have to deal with concrete situations in which very often we must be content to do what we *can*, not what we should choose to do if the situation were other than it is. The Christian must seek to discover the will of God not away from these limitations but inside them.[7]

E. G. Lee, speaking to the Church on "The Christian Failure," presents what amounts to a stinging challenge to the preacher-prophet. He says:

> The real aching challenge to the Christian religion in the modern world comes not so much from the criticism of thought as from the profound unhappiness of a morality that is not sanctioned by the current religion. The Church does not convincingly explain to mass-men how they should behave in the most intimate of their personal relations; in fact it is not too much to say that the Church has partly resigned from moral direction in these matters.[8]

The preacher-prophet, through participation in the making of moral decisions to do whatever "mass-man" *can* do in a particular concrete situation, can further mend the severed lines of communication with many of his hearers. Such a participation will inform them of his message today. Moreover, his presence and his own agony of mind and soul in moral decision-making with mass men will symbolize for them the relevancy and realism of Christianity's approach to the problems of their moral and spiritual life. This must indeed be one of the ways of God's

[7] F. R. Barry, *Recovery of Man*, Charles Scribner's Sons, 1949, pp. 49 f.
[8] *Mass Man and Religion*, Harper and Brothers, 1949, p. 39.

own Self-disclosure to contemporary man in mass society. This, even "hollow men," with but little interior substance and coherence and supported in the main by "external organization," can understand and profit by.

IV

A third reason for the breakdown in communication between the preacher-prophet and mass man and his turning away from the Church to find the real convictions of his life elsewhere is that many of the Christian concepts and ideas propounded from the pulpit are, in modern man's present condition, too advanced for his Christian experience. This means, as has already been suggested in another connection, that too much contemporary preaching starts at the wrong end. The preacher-prophet, committed as he is to the Christian ideals of love and the Kingdom of God, feels that he would be derelict in his duty and prophetic function if he failed to storm the very minds and consciences of men today with these ideals and concepts so valid for man in all times and so ultimate as spiritual ends.

The preacher-prophet must indeed remain faithful to the vision of God's Kingdom of love on earth and never compromise the absolute validity and ultimacy of this ideal. But he must recognize that he is advocating an ideal Christian life for man in his mass-produced contemporary existence, and that he is not being unfaithful to the ideal if he guides his hearers to achieve the ultimate in proximate steps.

Many persons today will respond wholeheartedly to a call for justice and freedom and equality of all peoples who will remain cold and unresponsive to a call to love all peoples. This unresponsiveness very often is viewed by the preacher-prophet as rebellious or sinful behavior. But, perhaps, just as often it is an indication of the spiritual immaturity on the part of many hearers who are quite capable of understanding and appreciating the concepts, for instance, of justice and community but not advanced enough spiritually to find in the ideals of love and the Kingdom of God sufficient incentive for moral courage and action. The motive for their action must be found in a more utilitarian purpose, in workable, even if proximate, programs of action. And the preacher-prophet must be willing to chance proclaiming a partial Gospel to give them moral and spiritual direction through concrete suggestions in his area of competence rather than through the preaching of abstract Christian ideas.

John the Baptist, for example, felt the necessity of giving to those of his hearers who were ready to give evidence of their repentance concrete things to do even though he had exhorted them to "bring forth therefore fruits worthy of repentance" (Luke 3:8).

> And the people asked him, saying, What shall we do then? He answereth and saith unto them, He that hath two coats, let him impart to him that hath none; and he that hath meat, let him do likewise. Then came also publicans to be baptized, and said unto him, Master, what shall we do? And he said unto them, Exact no more than that which is appointed you. And the soldiers likewise demanded of him, saying, And what shall we do? And he said unto them, Do violence to no man, neither accuse *any* falsely; and be content with your wages (Luke 3:10-14).

How much social concern and goodwill are wasted for the lack of concrete channels through which to express them! How many people who would live the good life turn disappointedly away from the Church because the moral and spiritual demands made upon them are greater than they at their level of spiritual development can fully meet!

But must they be turned away? Cannot the proclamation of the Word be "good news" to all of those who are out of communication with the Church through its preacher-prophet? The inherent optimism, persistency and creativity of the Christian faith have but one answer to each of these two questions.

V

The very genius and power of the Christian faith are in its creativity, in its capacity for thriving in any climate and for meeting with timely, yet eternal, competency the demands and exigencies and needs of any historical period. Its light may burn low but it never flickers out. The world of history and the word of the Bible is the same on this point: "The light still shines in the darkness, and the darkness has never put it out."[9] In the fullness of time or at the right moment, it bursts forth into full fluorescence.

The survival or rebirth of a civilization is contingent upon the applied genius of the Christian faith. It is this genius which gives the lie to the fatalism and pessimism of an Oswald Spengler who, viewing civilizations as living organisms and in terms of the four seasons of spring, summer, autumn and winter, asserted that every civilization moves inevitably from birth to death just as "an individual human being."[10] It is also the genius of the Christian faith to provide its thinkers and scholars with the necessary insight to see that, unlike a living organism, civilizations are dependent for their survival and growth or rebirth upon individual human beings and not upon human societies as organisms. Such a scholar is Arnold Joseph Toynbee. In making the individual human being's response to the challenges of his physical and human environments the vital force in the rise and growth or the decline and rebirth of a civilization, Toynbee is appropriating the insight of the Judaeo-Christian faith. He writes:

> The individual energies of all the human beings who constitute the so-called 'members' of a society are the vital forces whose operation works out the history of that society, including its time-span.[11]

And — with a moral and Christian note which grows increasingly louder in his epochal work:

> These individuals who set going the process of growth in the societies to which they "belong" are more than mere men. They

[9] John 1:5 (J. B. Phillips, *The New Testament in Modern English,* The Macmillan Company, 1952).

[10] *Decline of the West,* Knopf, 1926.

[11] *A Study of History,* abridgement of vols. 1-6 by D. C. Somervell, Oxford University Press, 1946, p. 248.

can work what to men seem miracles because they themselves are superhuman in a literal and no mere metaphorical sense.[12]

The Christian religion is a creative faith which works dynamically in a civilization through creative individual human beings. Inflexibility, stagnancy and decadence are disagreeable to it. When in its majority or dominant expression or organized form these things are evident, in its minority expression, its unorthodox and simply structured forms, it continues to be creative and deeply alive. It is this fact which brings hope to those hearers of the Word who would live the good life but cannot bring themselves to identify themselves with the inflexible, unimaginative and, to them, meaningless forms of Christianity as presently conceived and organized.

At the same time, however, this fact keeps a significant group of responsible and perceptive persons faithful to the Church and the Word and justifies their continued and avowed identification with the Church even when the traditional forms of its life and work have spent their force and lost their meaning for a vast number of people.

It is undoubtedly true, as E. G. Lee says, that the Church is no longer that "representative of a minority" which "always spoke for the mass." And it may be further said that the Church speaks today only for a segment and not the whole of its constituents. But this fact of itself should not alarm us into panic and convince us that the Church and the faith it represents is any nearer to its expiration than it was at the peak of its vitality and appeal. Its hope and future as well as the hope and future of a Christian civilization always reside in those responsible, perceptive and creative Christian individuals who are not afraid to create new and relevant forms of expression of the Christian faith through which to communicate the gospel to mass men; who are not so careful of the reputation of God that they, though with the best of intentions, underestimate His power "to do a new thing."

If many persons of the deepest integrity and human concern

12 *Ibid.*, p. 212.

and the highest idealism turn from the Church because their imagination and religious impulse are stirred more by a proposed Peace Corps, by sit-in demonstrations and the action programs of a labor union or a political party than by a sterile, undemanding program of the Church, it does not necessarily follow that these same persons could not be turned back to the Church with a risk-taking, energy-demanding, essential Christian program conceived, purposed and planned in terms both comprehensible and meaningful to this generation of our mass-produced contemporary life.

The appeal of contemporary programs, which are coming to mean a particular way of life to which many persons today are willing to commit themselves, lies in the fact that these programs are applicable to the areas of life where the crucial decisions of mass men are being made. They direct men to meet each other in what Martin Buber calls "the place of lived speech."[13] It is here that genuine communication may be known because the language spoken and the form in which it is used is "lived speech."

The Church through its preacher-prophets must not be unwilling to learn from the new social and political activity of emerging responsible collectivities how to reach vast numbers of mass men who are not now being reached with the gospel. Perhaps, in the process, it may also garner additional insights for presenting more effectively the gospel to those who are less demanding but manifestly in need of a revitalized and meaningful faith.

It must be pointed out here, however, that all of the prophets of meaning and significance to mass men are not outside of the Church. As a matter of fact, the ones currently holding the center of attention are representatives of the Church. Their activities are illustrative of the bold, new, and imaginative ways in which convictions of the Christian faith are being communicated to mass men. Many of them are hearing the voice of the

[13] Martin Buber, *Between Man and Man,* The Macmillan Company, 1947, p. 14.

Son of God through these preacher-prophets. And they are becoming witnesses of a new life in God through our Lord Jesus Christ.

To be sure, mass men who have turned from the Church to find the real convictions of the Christian faith elsewhere need not be permanently estranged from the Church and the historic Christian faith of which it is the custodian and chief interpreter. It is still, and continually, productive of a preacher-prophet and a creative Christian individual through whom the eternal and ever resurging vitalities of the Christian faith may be known and demonstrated, and bold, new, and imaginative experiments in the communication of the Gospel implemented.

VI

In the preceding section of this chapter we dealt with how man may be turned back to the Church for practical guidance by the preacher-prophet through his response to the challenge of man's contemporary condition. It remains now for us to discuss how the gospel may become "good news" to modern man in his predicament.

We may begin this discussion by asking: What is the challenge in man's contemporary condition to which, if the preacher-prophet responds wisely and appropriately to it, man may be brought convincingly to a profound conviction of the "good news" of the gospel? To ask the question is to spark not only original thinking on our part but to kindle a greater interest on our part in the acute and arresting analyses of contemporary man's condition available to us in the works of post-biblical thinkers from Nietzsche, Hegel, and Kierkegaard (and such of his successors as Karl Jasper, Jean-Paul Sartre and Gabriel Marcel) to Martin Heidegger and Paul Tillich.[14]

---

[14] The busy pastor or minister who is interested in furthering his acquaintance with the thought of the men whose names are listed here, and especially their insights into modern man's condition, will find greatly rewarding chapters 5-7 and the Epilogue of Stuart Barton Babbage's excellent little book *Man in Nature and in Grace,* Wm. B. Eerdmans Publishing Company, 1957. These are comprehensive, though concise

To ask the question is also to send us back with a more clearly defined purpose to a study of the Biblical writings about man, particularly those of the eighth-century prophets and of Paul[15] and we shall want seriously to study also the pertinent works of Augustine and Luther, Calvin and Pascal,[16] as well as those of Plato and Aristotle, "forerunners" of the gospel.

Contemporary man, in common with man in every age, has three basic urges to which the Gospel today must appeal: the urge *to do* (activity), the urge *to belong* (community), and the urge *to be* (authenticity). Having said this, two brief digressions must be made here immediately. The first is with reference to the order in which these urges are listed here.

It may be pointed out that the urge *to be* would seem to have logical priority over the other two. This is agreed. But psychologically the urge *to do* would seem to take priority. Mass man is a particularly active creature who today is caught up in a veritable vortex of external activity from which it seems impossible for him to extricate himself (even if he seriously wished to do so, in spite of his complaints that he is too busy). Activity is a level on which he immediately lives and which, this writer feels, is the first entrance to his basic need *to be.* Thus it is submitted here that the preacher-prophet who would really communicate the gospel to mass man should not look in anguish upon man's activity and thus proclaim: *"Be still."* Rather, he must proclaim: *"Be active."*

But the preacher-prophet will understand that, through his ministry of practical guidance, he will lead his mass-produced

chapters on "Man and Modern Existentialism," "Man and English Literature," and "Man and Human Mortality." It is not the writer's purpose to review the works of these men, only to point the reader to pertinent and fruitful sources of inquiry and knowledge on the subject under discussion.

[15] See Romans, chapters 1 and 7 for Paul's description of man's predicament.

[16] The busy preacher is again referred to Stuart Barton Babbage's book, *Man in Nature and in Grace,* chapter 3, which discusses "Man and Christian Thought." The reader need not to be reminded that all of the post-biblical writers referred to here — as well as pre-biblical writers — should be read and understood in the light of what the Bible says about man and his condition.

hearers *to be active* in essential, meaningful, and cosmically significant ways. So, as a matter of practical necessity, we should approach man first in response to his urge to do.[17]

The second brief digression concerns the basic urges of man himself. While contemporary man is a possessor of these urges, as is man in every era, his attempt to express them today is so conditioned by the mechanization of a technological civilization as to give them a radically different form, if not substance. The dominant factors involved in his historical existence are no longer congenial. They are for the most part negative factors which must be transformed into positive potentialities. In other words, contemporary man's experiences of estrangement, emptiness, anxiety, doubt, guilt, and awareness of "having to die"[18] must be transvalued into the immediate positives from which new life for him in an authentic existence may be created. For these experiences, as pointed out by Paul Tillich,[19] have a religious character. This character makes them positive potentialities.

Now we may continue with the gospel's appeal to modern man's basic urge *to do*.

It has already been pointed out that mass man is a creature of activity. He needs activity. He wants it, although he complains

[17] The same approach may be made to modern man's noisiness. He should not be told: "Keep quiet!" but: "Be noisy!" But having told him to be noisy, the preacher-prophet will, through practical guidance, show him what to be noisy about. When man becomes loudly insistent about the right things, about things which are truly and patently important to his authentic self, he will be quiet when the demand for loud insistence is absent in a given situation.

[18] See the following on the significance of human death in contradistinction to death as a biological fact: Paul Tillich, *Systematic Theology*, The University of Chicago Press, Vol. 2, 1957, pp. 72 f.; Martin Heidegger, *Existence and Being*, Henry Regnery Company, 1950; and Reinhold Niebuhr, *The Nature and Destiny of Man*, Charles Scribner's Sons, 1949, Vol. 2, p. 293.

[19] *Op. cit.*, Part III, chapter 1, *passim*. See also Paul Tillich, *The Courage To Be*, Yale University Press, 1952, as a reference for this entire concluding discussion, although the writer does not intend what he says in these final pages to be in any way a discussion of the views contained in this book.

about being "too busy." His dilemma inheres in the fact that he needs and wants activity, but he is too often active in the wrong things, and things, at that, which he himself has had no real part in purposing or planning. He is called upon to act upon matters, and in ways concerning which someone else has made the decisions, determined the plan of action, and set the goals.

To be sure, contemporary man is called upon to participate in programs of action which must be determined on the basis of technical knowledge which is not available to him. But the general character of our mechanized life leaves little room for personal participation in basic policy- and decision-making today. Man must content himself to act automatically in many situations and without the benefit of having been involved personally in a group-thinking process.

Moreover, too many of the activities in which mass man is involved fall into the category of "busy work" — mere activity because he must be active. He gives himself to all kinds of meaningless activities. He becomes the International Vice-president of the Society To Keep Moose in the Northern Part of the State! He consistently attends all of the civic meetings, leaving one before the business of the day is called for and arriving at another after the business of the day has been transacted. And when the day is over, he is tired and tries to rest so that he may be fresh for such engagements the next day.

But mass man needs more than mere activity — a frustrating, enervating kind of business. He needs involvement in an activity which is demanding, dangerous, and crucial because of its essentiality and urgency.

Man in any age, but especially mass man, grows weary of an activity in which there is no real challenge and demand, which does not involve him in crucial, personal decision-making or which does not offer him hard and urgently necessary things to do. Without difficulty man will lapse into laziness, and, having become indolent, will require difficulty to keep him intellectually, morally and spiritually free.

This thought has been remarkably expressed by Kierkegaard:

I had been a student for ten years. Although never lazy, all of my activity nevertheless was like a glittering inactivity, a kind of occupation for which I still have a strong predilection, and perhaps even a little talent....

Among other thoughts I remember this: "You are now," I said to myself, "on the way to becoming an old man, without being anything, and without really undertaking to do anything. On the other hand, wherever you look about you, in literature and in life, you see the celebrated names and figures, the precious and much heralded men who are coming into prominence and are much talked about, the many benefactors of the age who know how to benefit mankind by making life easier and easier, some by railways, others by omnibuses and steamboats, others by telegraph, others by easily apprehended compendiums and short recitals of everything worth knowing, and finally the true benefactors of the age who by virtue of thought make spiritual existence systematically easier and easier, and yet more and more significant. And what are you doing?"...and then suddenly there flashed through my mind this thought: "You must do something, but inasmuch as with your limited capacities it will be impossible to make anything easier than it has become, you must, with the same humanitarian enthusiasm as the others, undertake to make something harder." This notion pleased me immensely, and at the same time it flattered me to think that I, like the rest of them, would be loved and esteemed by the whole community. For when all combine in every way to make everything easier and easier, there remains only one possible danger, namely, that the easiness might become so great that it would be too great; then only one want is left, thought not yet a felt want — that people will want difficulty.[20]

Contemporary man needs difficulty today in his urge *to do*. The difficulty of the sort required to appeal to this basic urge is a quality and challenge of the Christian faith, pre-eminently symbolized by the cross of Christ. For the cross is no perverted symbol of the temptations and hardships, the pain and suffering "common to man." The depth of its meaning may be found in the temptation in the wilderness when Jesus made the personal and deliberate choice to make His appeal to man on the basis of man's basic, though many times slowly recognized, needs rather

[20] From "Concluding Unscientific Postscript," *A Kierkegaard Anthology*, edited by Robert Bretall, Princeton University Press, 1946, pp. 193 f.

than in terms of what man immediately feels and wants. It is also found in the Transfiguration, where again He makes a personal decision to scorn danger and sacrifice to pursue His chosen course, even though the knowledge of the personal cost to Moses of leading the children of Israel to the Promised Land and to Elijah of contending that "Jehovah is God" was known to Him.

The courage of the cross is different in kind from the instinctive courage one shows when risking personal danger to rescue a person trapped in a house on fire or to snatch a child from the path of a speeding vehicle. It is the courage, born of a deliberate, voluntary personal decision and choice, to make even the supreme sacrifice for Jesus' sake. One makes this choice with one's eyes wide open and with full knowledge of the cost involved in one's personal decision and commitment. No greater challenge and opportunity *to do* can be offered to modern man than those offered by the Christian faith today to "hate evil" (Ps. 97:10), to "come out" from among the wicked and be... "separate" (II Cor. 6:17), and to "come...deny himself, and take up his cross, and follow" Christ (Matt. 16:24).

Nothing can offer man today more challenge and danger, more opportunity for essential and cosmically significant service, more urgently necessary activity than the call of the Judaeo-Christian faith "to root out, and to pull down, and to destroy, and to throw down, to build, and to plant" (Jer. 1:10). It is the preacher-prophet's task to lead modern man to such an encounter through the gospel.

VII

The gospel makes an appeal also to the basic urge of mass man *to belong*. This is a basic urge because its fulfillment is a metaphysical requirement. Man seeks a footing and standing in his group ultimately not because of his vanity or his will to power or his will to dominate but because of his will *to be*. For it is only in direct, meaningful relationships with other individual selves that a man can know himself to be an individual self. True organic community individuates him. He is made aware that he is an individual but an incomplete individual in spite of all his individual wholeness. Individuation stresses his consciousness of *being one* but his consciousness of *needing others* as well. "None of us liveth to himself," says Paul (Rom. 14:7). "No man is an Iland intire of it selfe," John Donne reminds us.[21]

Man's natural form for transcending the inadequacy of his singularity is communication. Thus in order to fulfill his basic urge *to belong* he becomes a communicating self. This communication is not always with words. It is "lived speech," to use Buber's phrase again. It is an unspoken acceptance, a felt "at-homeness" with others, a dynamic relationship of honesty, truth, and mutuality. Communication is direct and, hence, personal. It is essential, hence, authentic.

Communication must always be the precondition of community and a sense of common, shared concerns must be its basis. But the source and the possibility of community must be sought in the *face-value* person — the person whose external expressions correspond with the inner truth of what he really is. The association of any other kind of person is deceitful, schismatic, and anarchic.

Contemporary man finds it difficult to achieve community because the conditions under which he lives and works are not congenial to the fulfillment of his urge *to belong*. Technological civilization of which he is a product is too mechanical, proliferating, immediate, and soulless to be a natural habitat for the flowering of his spirit and the creation of organic community. He can *belong* only in an organic community because his sense of belonging must coincide with his sense of being bound to others. And this awareness dictates that the form and expression of his authentic belonging will be his assumption of personal responsibility in the group.

Man is never so responsible as when he belongs. And he

[21] *Complete Poetry and Selected Prose of John Donne* and *Complete Poetry of William Blake*, ed. John Hayward and Geoffrey Keynes, Random House, 1941, p. 332.

never belongs quite so authentically as when he is responsible. This is the essence of community.

Man's assumption of personal responsibility, it must be said, should be first of all in response to his acknowledged accountability to God, his Creator and Redeemer. Allan A. Zaun, minister of the Jefferson Avenue Presbyterian Church, Detroit, Michigan, has made the following comment in discussion with the writer on this point:

> Why should man feel responsible at all? Is it not because he is responsible first of all to God? For, apart from God, a man has no real responsibility to his fellows. It is this "vertical" dimension, I suggest, that is prior to the "horizontal". I love my neighbor because God loves him. Otherwise humanism is completely true.

Quite so! And this makes authentic community a quite different thing from the movement and behavior of individuals *en masse* who feel no real need for personal decision or freedom to be responsible; who evidence no penitence for the crimes and evils which they as individuals *en masse* commit.

Although it is difficult for mass man to achieve community in modern industrialized society, he may yet find the source of power and the guidance in the Christian faith for overcoming this difficulty. It was Paul who reminded Christian believers and seekers after the faith in an alien world that "our commonwealth is in heaven, and from it we await a Saviour, the Lord Jesus Christ" (Phil. 3:20; RSV).

But this is a "commonwealth" with an earthly counterpart in the Church, and not simply the Church understood as an organization or institution of the Christian faith. It is the Church living as *the* fellowship of faith which, in truth, is *the* fellowship of the cross. The person who seeks really *to belong* today must turn to that fellowship which has "all things in common" under the watchful ministries which God in Christ Jesus has ordained —

> for building up the body of Christ, until we all attain to the unity of the faith and of the knowledge of the Son of God, to mature manhood, to the measure of the stature of the fulness of Christ; so that we may no longer be children, tossed to and fro and carried about with every wind of doctrine, by the cunning of

men, by their craftiness in deceitful wiles. Rather, speaking the truth in love, we are to grow up in every way into him who is the head, into Christ, from whom the whole body, joined and knit together by every joint with which it is supplied, when each part is working properly, makes bodily growth and upbuilds itself in love (Eph. 4:12-16; RSV).

Thus the judgment of the Christian faith is that mass man needs community which is more than a loose association for "fun and fellowship" or even a cover for his impenitence and irresponsibility. He needs community which is a noble, individuating, personal, power-releasing, and basic-urge-fulfilling bondage. He needs community which is the essence of belonging. This is pre-eminently the potentiality of the Christian faith, with which mass man may become acquainted through the gospel.

VIII

Finally, the gospel may appeal to the basic urge of mass man *to be* (authenticity). Mass man is not what God, his Creator, intended him to be. Estranged from God, he is a sinner. Involved in the processes of a machine civilization, he is in danger of becoming no more than a "cog" in its gigantic mass operations; he is in danger of becoming a sub-man in the mechanical atmosphere of contemporary civilization.

With profound insight into the condition of contemporary man, T. S. Eliot writes:

> *The desert is not remote in southern tropics,*
> *The desert is not only around the corner,*
> *The desert is squeezed in the tube-train next to you,*
> *The desert is in the heart of your brother.*[22]

And again:

> *We are the hollow men*
> *We are the stuffed men*
> *Leaning together*
> *Headpiece filled with straw. Alas!*
> *Our dried voices, when*
> *We whisper together*

[22] *Collected Poems* of T. S. Eliot, Harcourt, Brace and Company, 1930, p. 182.

> Are quiet and meaningless
> As wind in dry grass
> Or rat's feet over broken glass
> In our dry cellar.
> Shape without form, shade without colour,
> Paralysed force, gesture without motion;
> Those who have crossed
> With driest eye, to death's other Kingdom
> Remember us — if at all — not as lost
> Violent souls, but only
> As the hollow men
> The stuffed men.[23]

This is death to the "living soul" into whose nostrils God has breathed "the breath of life." The breath of God is the oxygen of the soul and without its supply the soul dies. This is in effect what technological civilization does to man. It cuts him off from the "native air" of the soul. It "undermines" his moral and spiritual order and leaves him unrelated to his world and himself, and alienated from the Power which created him.

Mass man is a symbol of this estrangement and death. And yet he is not absolutely dead. Herein is the source of his anguish, dread, and despair. He is the creature possessing "immortal longings," who believes "he was not made to die." Yet his unauthentic existence in mass society is a negation of his authentic self which he of necessity wills to become.

But what is it to be an authentic self? Or, put another way, what is it *to be*? Three brief comments are submitted here.

The first comment has to do with a definition of existence. Babbage reminds us that the word "existence" comes from the Latin verb *existere,* which means "to step forth, as in personal decision."[24] To be in existence, therefore, is to be engaged with all one's being in personal decision-making. It is to move with impassioned deliberation toward a definite *standpoint* because that particular standpoint is morally and spiritually decisive for the person who chooses it. When one meets "the moment to

---

[23] *Ibid.,* p. 101.
[24] *Op. cit.,* p. 68. See also Paul Tillich, *Systematic Theology,* Vol. 2, pp. 19-21.

decide" with the courage to make a decision for oneself and to act out this courage in an act of personal decision, one exists.

The second comment relates to the necessity of direct personal experience in authentic existence. The self is a reflection of other selves, indeed it is no authentic self at all, when it is moved only by the strings of another's mind. If it must live only on the impact of the ideational activity of another and experience only vicariously the real issues of its existence, it must be doomed to unauthenticity.

But mass man as an individual self cannot, for all of "the desert" in his heart, submit to a negation of himself by mass society. He must act for himself, and on his own. This is the basic meaning of the Greek noun from which the English adjective "authentic" is derived: *authentes,* meaning, "one who does things oneself."

A third comment deals with the substance or the content of the self. Kierkegaard speaks of the self as being "a synthesis of the infinite and the finite, of the temporal and the eternal."[25] It is of these two possible sources of *human* experience that the content of the self is formed. It becomes subject to despair (Kierkegaard's word for *sin*) when it is lacking either in finitude or infinitude. It is lacking in finitude when it resists returning from moments and heights of rapture in its response to the reality of infinity to its finite plane of life's daily and necessary tasks. This refusal to return to ourselves, to finitude, says Kierkegaard, establishes a disrelationship and constitutes a form of (unconscious) despair.

The self is lacking in infinitude when it lives only on a plane of "immediacy" or finitude as though there were nothing higher to reach for or anything more precious to value. An existence on the level of "immediacy" is a state of worldliness. And about this state Kierkegaard has said: "Worldliness means precisely attributing infinite value to things indifferent."[26]

---

[25] Soren Kierkegaard, *The Sickness Unto Death,* Princeton University Press, 1941, Reprinted, A Doubleday Anchor Book, p. 146.

[26] *Ibid.,* p. 166.

The authentic self is volatilized by too much infinitude and is defrauded of its substance by too much finitude. Either causes the *despair* (sin) which negates the authentic self; it cannot fulfill its urge *to be*. A disrelationship exists between it and God before whom it is a self.

Mass man is a self filled with too much of the world, the temporal, the finite; he does not find the source of his despair in too much of the infinite. The kingdom of this world (the kingdom of worldliness of the abundance and supremacy of things obtainable in this world) is his contemporary state of being — a state characterized by estrangement and despair. His despair, understood theologically, is sin or corruption in the soul. From the body of this death (worldliness), he cannot deliver himself in order to be what he needs to become *before God*. He needs the gospel, whether he is conscious of this need or not.

The gospel must show him the way to deliverance through repentance and faith in Jesus Christ our Lord. Since he can be what he ought to be only before God, the reconciling power of the gospel must transform his disrelationship with God to one of fellowship with God through Christ. Living in fellowship with God in Christ is to be spiritual and to live the life of the Spirit. And to be spiritual is to be authentic.

IX

Since appealing to mass man's urge *to be* is making an appeal to the most advanced religious conception of which he is capable, the preacher-prophet will understand the practical necessity of first establishing communication with him on the lower levels of his experience. Fulfilling the urge *to be* is contemporary man's most pressing need, but the "good news" of this possibility must be brought to him on successive and ascending levels of spiritual communication. What does it matter if the gospel comes first of all as a faint voice whispering in his ear if, in time, it may become a trumpet blast in his soul?

CHAPTER FOUR

God's Voice in Community Affairs

The preacher-prophet's concern with the moral and spiritual problems of organized human life reaches back to the settling of the Israelite clans in the hill country of Canaan and their eventual coalescense with the Amorites who inhabited the walled cities in the lowlands of this new land into which the Israelites had come. The Israelite clans came out of the desert conditioned by and committed to a kinship or brother-justice. The circumstances of nomadic life had taught them the necessity of holding a given territory or district as a common possession, of moving about together in search of food or for purposes of defense, and of sharing the fortune or misfortune of the clan as a common lot.

The preserving quality of their clan life had inhered in the diligent practice of justice among its own members on terms dictated to them by the desert. The persisting question of judgment upon the clan's every act and practice had become: Is this act or practice brotherly? This *mishpat*, to use the Hebrew term, had become identified with the will of Jahweh who had brought them out of the land of Egypt and across the Red Sea.

It is both interesting and significant that the Hebrew term *mishpat* (translated "judgment" in the KJV and "justice" in the ARV and the RSV) as used in its many connections in the Old Testament admits more than a merely personal interpretation. The term also translates "law," "legal right," "custom," "manner," "ordering," and so forth. It may therefore be understood to refer to the ethical and social arrangements or a legal system according to which human life is organized and ordered. The wandering clans of Israel had ordered their lives according to *mishpat,* which was not only well suited to nomadic life but which was founded upon principles of enduring value.[1] They asked: Is my individual conduct as a clan member brotherly? Are our clan arrangements brotherly? It is true, the application of these principles did not extend beyond clan life. The universal application of these principles had yet to be conceived, which, indeed, in time it was.

When the Israelite clans ceased to be a society *in motion,* in the desert, and became a society *at rest,* in the land of an advanced people with a commercial civilization, they found themselves confronted with the problem of resolving a fundamental difference between nomadism and civilization. They had now to address themselves to the question: Under the new and different circumstances of civilization, what is just and what is right? What is brotherly? It was the true prophets of Jahweh whose voices contributed most significantly toward an early answer to this question.

I

Seen from this perspective the true prophet belies an ancient common notion that prophecy is equated with prediction and that the prophet is concerned only with the "things to come." The true prophet is, and always has been, a spokesman for God. His primary function as understood by the Hebrew term *nabi,* the Greek verb *keryssein,* and his historic role is that of proclaiming God's word of warning, judgment, and hope. The essential nature of his work is preaching — that of proclaiming

---

[1] For a full and scholarly discussion of the sociological interpretation of the development of the Hebrew nation and ethic, the reader is referred to Louis Wallis, *Sociological Study of the Bible,* University of Chicago Press, 1912. The present writer reflects the standpoint of this book in the first whole section of this chapter. His debt to the author is here freely acknowledged.

God's timeless Word delivered to him to the people of his own generation.

Moreover, this timeless Word of God is always directed through His spokesman to persons in their ethical and social relationships — relationships which constitute the social arrangements or structure within which human life is organized. There are copious and outstanding illustrations of this truth in the Bible.

Samuel foresaw the evils which would result from the political arrangements of the monarchy Israel insisted upon establishing. That these political arrangements under Saul, their first king, were not brotherly in the light of desert *mishpat* is borne out by the Biblical record. It is recorded that when David, in his flight from Saul, escaped to the cave Adullam, he was there joined by "everyone that was in distress, and everyone that was in debt, and everyone that was discontented" in the hill-country kingdom under Saul (I Sam. 22:2).

Political arrangements grew progressively worse under David and Solomon. Their governments were convulsed by uprisings of the peasantry. They were maintained only with the aid of hired soldiers, referred to in the Hebrew as *gibberim* and translated "mighty men." The use of mercenaries by the government, although a common practice of the times, was fiercely condemned by the later prophets. Hosea proclaimed: "Thou didst trust in thy way, in the multitude of thy mighty men" (Hos. 10:13). Isaiah announced: "For behold, the Lord, the Lord of hosts, doth take away from Jerusalem, and from Judah...the mighty man, and the man of war" (Isa. 3:1, 2).

Elijah came forth from the hill country of Gilead to condemn King Ahab for seizing Naboth's land. The conspiracy Elijah condemned involved murder which had been given a legal form by "the elders and the nobles" who constituted the court to which Naboth was answerable.

The prophets spoke out in the name of Jahweh against the oppressive economic and social arrangements of the nation and the partial and corrupt administration of justice through the courts. They pleaded for righteousness and social justice — for obedience to the Lord their God. "Let justice well up as waters," cried Amos, "and righteousness as a mighty stream" (Amos 5:24). Micah proclaimed: "He has showed you, O man, what is good; and what does the Lord require of you but to do justice, and to love kindness, and to walk humbly with your God" (Micah 6:8, RSV). And thus spoke the Master: "Thou shalt love the Lord thy God with all thy heart, and with all thy soul, and with all thy mind. This is the first and great commandment. And the second is like unto it, Thou shalt love thy neighbour as thyself. On these two commandments hang all the law and the prophets" (Matt. 22:37-40).

Thus the preacher-prophet today who concerns himself with the ethical and social relationships of organized community life as a spokesman for God stands in the best tradition of the true prophets of old and follows in the footsteps of his Lord and Master, Jesus Christ.

For his concern with community affairs today, however, the preacher-prophet will not find in Biblical literature modern concepts of community living, but he will, nevertheless, discover there profound insights for dealing with community problems. He will find no concrete social programs to offer the community, but there will be challenge and inspiration aplenty for the collective achievement of justice, public order, and love in this Book.[2] Thus the preacher-prophet is not without a role or

[2] Too frequently many who look in vain for a concrete social program in the Bible underestimate the importance of Biblical passages which do contain valuable social insights for today's living. One such passage is Luke 3:10-14, cited in Chapter 2. This passage records the answer of John the Baptist to those of his hearers who would follow some specific and concrete course of action to prove their repentance: The *multitudes* were directed to share what they possessed. The *publicans* were counseled to be just and fair with those of whom they could easily take advantage. And the soldiers were enjoined to be non-violent, just, and honest, in their work and content with their pay, lest they extort from those over whom they had authority and hence an advantage.

In each case, John the Baptist related his hearers' social duty to their personal ability. Their specific responsibilities were dictated not only by their personal ability but by their opportunities as well. They were not

a message in community affairs. Let us now look at his respon-
sibilty in several important areas of community concern.

II

First of all, let us consider the problem of the individual
citizen's conception of his relationship to the community. Not
too many years ago Lewis Gannett wrote a book entitled *Cream
Hill*. In this book he tells us that, though bound by necessity to
the city from Monday to Friday, his weekends the year round
are spent in the country. During this two-day period, he seeks
another mode of existence through country living. Living in
the country on Saturday and Sunday makes city living tolerable
for him from Monday through Friday. But he reflects that in
giving himself to this mode of existence he is evading his responsibility as a citizen of the city. He is not available to accept
any serious responsibilities or social duties in the city or the
country. He leaves evil to increase without protest in the city
and undermines the strength of country life by non-participation.
He is responsible nowhere.

Lewis Gannett focuses upon a very serious problem in our
community life. His whole reflection assumes that the individual
citizen is the source and subject of a responsible and healthy
community life; that it is his decisions and choices upon which
public policy is based and community affairs conducted; and that
the support of public policies once enacted into law as well as
support for community affairs wisely administered must come from
him. But he indicts himself and many other individual citizens
for community irresponsibility and a lack of appreciation of the
individual citizen's relationship to the community and its
processes.

But this situation to which Gannett refers is not true only
of those who escape the city on week-ends or every evening after

directed nor expected to do what they did not have the ability or the
opportunity to do. John the Baptist's insights in this passage reveal an
enduring principle which can be applied by anyone or any group in
any age.

working hours for that matter. It is true of a vast number of individual citizens who take the community for granted and proceed to live their individual lives as though it did not exist. Entangling their lives with artificial relationships, they fail to participate in or to influence the real and heterogeneous life of an organic community.

Organic community life and its processes suggests a proximity and social intercourse with many persons of a diversity of abilities and skills, "accents and tastes". It requires the responsibly concerned individual citizen to accept the inconveniences and unpleasantries, the aggravations and the sometimes gruelling labor inherent in the proximity and social intercourse of organic community life and to enter into creative tension with other community members in this heterogeneous situation. It reveals the logic — and the necessity — of the individual member's being influenced and guided in organization and community decision and action by the real needs and crucial issues found and felt by the group, and the worthy ends for which organic community groups should strive.

When citizens in the community organize themselves into groups over which they have complete control and around ends and purposes which they have created in order to give some logic to the organization and to maintain a comradery based on similar accents and tastes, they are ignoring, and actually working against, the genuine processes of organic community life to the extent that they give themselves only to such groups.

Generally such groups are characterized by real needs unrealistically met and false activity which engages the members in a busy work program. (This, of course, is characteristic of mass society, hence mass man.) While offering some personal satisfaction produced by their exclusiveness, by the false status they represent, by the confirmation of the group's intellectual and social prejudices, and by a convenience and ease which comes from a lack of encounter with the more disturbing elements in the total (organic) community life, such groups do not ultimately bring satisfaction to the individual member or a deeper meaning to his personal existence. They do not contribute significantly to the real needs and worthy ends of organic community life.

This fact is often overlooked by many well-meaning citizens of the community. While not joining the great exodus to the suburbs, some middle class citizens, for example, have made of the new and higher priced housing in areas of redevelopment in the city a virtual colony of families of similar orientation, tastes, and social interests, thereby practicing exclusiveness without always being aware of it. Some churches have followed their parishioners to the suburbs not because there was no longer any reason for their existence where they were but because their present location would involve them in a type and kind of ministry radically different from the one in which they had historically been engaged. Some individual citizens have overburdened themselves with memberships in a variety of secret and social clubs, convincing themselves that the purposes which they have created for such groups are genuine and worthy enough to deserve their greatest loyalty and support.

The withdrawal of responsible and capable citizens from the center of community life is an important factor in the deterioration of the community and its resources. The greater the withdrawal, in distance and interest, the more accelerated becomes the process of deterioration. And it is under such conditions that delinquency and crime, ennui and frustration thrive at that point in the city where we can least afford to have these things exist — at its very heart!

In a situation like this the preacher-prophet is under obligation to inform and to inspire the conscience of the community. Certainly, he is under constraint to inform the consciences of those who embrace the faith which he represents. For only when the conscience is informed are people impelled to relate themselves responsibly to the community and to be sober and wise in the decisions and choices they make. Only then do they work to achieve the possession of their own soul or to become an authentic self.

The complexities and demands of community living in modern industrialized society meet us wherever we are and wherever we go. The geographical location of the simple community life is hard to find. Quiet Haven soon becomes a new housing development with houses row on row and Shady Glen becomes the city of a new outlying factory. We are now forced to live with the complexities of community life and to meet its demands everywhere.

But this situation poses for us not only a sociological problem, but a spiritual problem as well. We must come to terms with it *spiritually* as well as sociologically. The fact of the crowded city sprawling out into metropolitanism with its complex organizational structure and the omni-present automobile are very real external facts. But may not another fact be that we mass-produced individuals feel overcrowded outside because we are over-crowded inside; that deterioration takes place outside of us because it had its beginning inside of us in the form of despair?

Thus here are two facts: the external fact of things about us and the internal fact of our own spiritual condition. Both must be considered in whatever we do to live with the complexities of modern industrialized society. There is a Chinese proverb which says that there are five and not four points on a compass: North, South, East, West, *and the point where you are*. So we ourselves are important in working our way out of any problem, whatever it is.

The lady who cracked her front door in response to a knock by a caller who turned out to be a settlement-house worker summarily dismissed him with the words: "Me and my husband ain't interested in nothin'." But the lady in the upstairs apartment was interested in something. She gave evidence of this: Her door yielded widely to the settlement-house worker's knock. The shades at her windows were raised evenly to let the sunshine in and to give an impression of neatness and orderliness. Her windows were opened to let the fresh air in. And one of those window sills was graced with a small pot holding a single geranium in full bloom.

We never lose a problem in a chase, or by being interested in nothing. All of the artificial relationships or the mental-escape hatches we contrive cannot make the complexities and demands of organic community living any less real and persistent. Neither can our oversimplification of community problems eliminate our need — and the demand — for involvement in a rigorous group thinking process for the purpose of solving these problems and meeting real community needs.

How frequently we are bedeviled by an oversimplified approach to problems in all areas of our common life. A review of some of the solutions to mass-societal living we commonly hear will reveal how ludicrous oversimplification can become.

Consider what is offered to correct our school situation: There's nothing wrong with our schools that cannot be corrected with more money, better teachers, free lunches, more milk, a new principal, the Three R's, or an active PTA.

With regard to our community situation, we hear: There's nothing wrong with our communities that cannot be corrected by more block clubs and community councils, more recreation for youth or better pay for policemen.

We hear with regard to our work situation: There's nothing wrong with our work situation that cannot be corrected by better pay checks, more help or personnel, more up-to-date equipment, a little more recognition, a change in attitude of those who work with us, a more considerate boss, or longer coffee breaks.

With regard to our family situation, we hear: There's nothing wrong with our family situation that cannot be corrected by more use of the woodshed for unruly children, better television programs, stricter censorship of movies and literature for children, more time-saving appliances, another car, more mothers at home, a Bible on the table, a new house, a new husband or a new wife.

And with respect to our churches, we hear: There's nothing wrong with our churches that cannot be corrected by more Bible preaching, the old-time religion, a bigger church building, an inclusive membership, larger attendance at the midweek prayer meeting, or tithing.

We must be willing to be honest with ourselves and with God and say: The problems we face, O God, are wide and deep. They are not only outside of us but in us. They reveal a deep-furrowed crisis in the whole of our personal and social life. Their solution requires a fundamental change in us and in society.

These changes cannot all be effected by hard and clever thinking, by city-planning or by exerting pressure at the right time upon the right persons. Beyond what we can wisely and effectively do to help ourselves, we must rely upon the power of the Holy Spirit who alone can change a heart of stone into a heart of flesh and give us the wisdom and courage and endurance to live creatively in and through all the complexities of our modern life. Only the Holy Spirit can give us a cloistered heart to shut us in from the noise of "selfish strife" and to shut out all that would prevent us from being calm in our souls.

Our greatest challenge and greatest opportunity is where we are.

Lift up thine eyes from the place where thou art and look... (Gen. 12:14-8), for the ground on which thou standest is holy ground (Josh. 5:15).

There is one more remark to be made in this connection. It concerns what our Lord and Saviour promises us for meeting the problems of our daily existence: "Come unto me," He says, "all ye who toil and are burdened, and I will give you rest" (Matt. 11:28, RSV). But let us be clear on the kind of rest He promises. The Greek word, *anapausis*, which is translated "rest" or "refresh" in our English Bible, means a temporary rest as preparation for future toil. What our Saviour promises us then is time to catch our breath; He promises us "a pause for a moment or two" in the midst of life's struggle before we are called to take up the struggle again. This is the nature of Christian rest in this world; and he who seeks something else shall surely be disappointed.

Moreover, the preacher-prophet today is obliged to remind the individual citizen in our mass society that the increasing role of public and private agencies in community life does not relieve him of personal responsibility. The injunction is still directed to him to feed the hungry, clothe the naked, care for the widows and orphans, lift up the fallen, and to champion the cause of the oppressed and underprivileged. These agencies represent the extended personal and moral responsibility the individual citizen owes to the collective (organic) life of which he is a part. Responsibility must always be *personally* felt.

Feeling community responsibility *personally* is not easy to achieve in our highly complex and industrialized society. Many forces of our machine culture militate against it. The ends of efficiency, and of producing the greatest quantities at the lowest cost and the highest returns, have caused us to place organization and automation high up on our scale of values in modern industrialized society, although these things are quite capable of becoming insidious disvalues. But we must organize (or is the word "overorganize"?), not realizing that the more organization we have the more remote becomes the center of our original concern and, hence, the group members' sense of personal responsibility.

Community responsibility becomes in time a bureaucratic function not infrequently performed by professional automatons. This is not always true, but it is always possible of becoming true in mass society.

The individual citizen can feel personally responsible in community affairs only when the "gatekeepers" interpret his organic relationship to community life, and encourage him to sustain it. Organic community life is never homogeneous, with unity in the sense of *conformity* as its goal. It is always heterogeneous, with unity in the sense of community as its goal. There is of necessity both diversity and pluralism in organic community life.[3] And the grand and essential effort of each citizen is to live in such a diverse and pluralistic community with appreciation and a sense of personal responsibility for each and all. Inorganic

[3] The reference here is to those societies which are made up of a number of different ethnic and cultural groups.

community relationships are artificial, unchallenging, and ultimately meaningless. Such relationships are really community
dis-relationships. And the individual who is involved in them
is to the extent of his involvement alienated from the source of
his own full life — his organic community; he is in dis-relation-
ship with his community and himself.

We must always be careful to see that what we effect as sound
and efficient organization is not in fact an artificial arrangement
aimed at achieving homogeneity, indeliberate conformity, and
exclusiveness.

The other value of high standing in our industrialized society
is automation. This is a machine process which accomplishes
with a few the work which previously had been done by many
human hands and minds. The output is greater than that of
which man without the benefit of this process is capable. The
product is often more accurate and uniform, if not a source of
human incentive and personal satisfaction.

The nature of the process involves the human worker as a part
of the process. In time he loses the meaning of his work, if not
work itself. He is no longer related as a person (worker) to a
product which will reflect the quality of his skill and the mark
of his own personality.

The effect that this process has upon the worker, the factory
worker particularly, is evidenced in the wider relationships of
citizen with citizen. Moreover, the qualities of this process invade
the minds of individual citizens and thus become a part of their
everyday relationships. Personal responsibility in community
affairs has now been greatly attenuated, if not lost, through a
common practice of referring persons in need or with problems
in need of solution to some organized agency established for
the welfare of the community. The practice of referral is proper
where a citizen recognizes the problem to be too specialized for
him or too large for him to handle alone. But when a citizen,
referring a matter or a person to the proper agency, refers also
his own responsibility — thereby relieving himself of any further
personal responsibility in the matter — he is unconsciously acting

under the influence of the process of automation, and not as an enlightened authentic citizen who feels his community responsibility *personally*.

All of this, of course, means that the preacher-prophet must inspire individual citizens and groups of individual citizens to apply the insights, judgments, and values of their religious faith to community processes and achievements. There will be many others to provide the tools and the skills with which the individual citizen must assume community responsibility. But the preacher-prophet must help him to will to serve, to dream the right dreams, to see visions of what ought to be, and to possess an undiscourageable faith without which no work, however worthy, can be nobly and effectively done.

III

Next let us consider the preacher-prophet and the many voices that are heard in the community. It is to be expected that many voices will be raised in the community on any community issue. The fact that voices are raised in response to an issue means that some voices will be in conflict because an issue implies conflict. While some voices that are heard will represent legitimate standpoints which need to be taken into account in the making of any community policy, yet other voices are those of the apostles of anger and discord, prejudice and hate. They should be recognized for what they are and strongly repulsed.

Legitimate voices in conflict produce a creative tension when an objective thinking process is possible. This is both healthy and constructive. But the voice of anger and discord, prejudice and hate is the voice of evil and destruction. It offers unwise counsel to the law-abiding citizen, and is a detriment to public order.

The preacher-prophet sees that even those voices representative of legitimate standpoints may inadvertently become obstructive to their own cause and thus injurious to the community itself. When responsible champions of legitimate standpoints employ the very methods and tactics they resist in their opponents to achieve their admittedly good objectives, they, themselves, have become irresponsible and injurious to the good ends they seek. If they will not admit the legitimacy and soundness of other points of view, if they by subtlety or intimidation seek to suppress any voice which is not in total agreement with their own, if they use unfair means to regiment all minds to their way of thinking, they have been entrapped by the same evils they so stoutly resist.

In such a situation the rank and file often become either too disturbed or too diffident to seek and to know the truth. They acquiesce in an evil which can only result in more evil. They are victims of the despair of weakness (in the Kierkegaardian sense).

The preacher-prophet must proclaim against this evil and plead that voices which speak in support of legitimate causes speak soberly, constructively, and fairly so that their own good ends may be soberly, constructively, and fairly achieved.

The voice of the preacher-prophet admittedly is only one amongst many voices in the community. But there is a difference. His is the voice of God when he speaks insightfully and profoundly to the spiritual condition of the community and its spiritual destiny.

He should recognize, moreover, that no serious objection is raised against his voice so long as it is in agreement with the dominant voice in the community. When his voice is in such agreement it is accepted as authentic. But when it is in conflict with the dominant voice being raised in the community, then he may be accused of interfering in matters beyond his depth, if not of being a false prophet.

At least two things should be observed here. In the first place, the true prophet of Jehovah was in constant conflict with the false prophet of his day who always spoke what the people wanted to hear. The false prophet's counsel, like that of Ahithophel's, "was as if a man had inquired at the oracle of God" (II Sam. 16:23). Although he was a voice speaking false prophecies to the people, yet he spoke with the authority and the assurance of the voice of God.

Doubtless many false prophets such as Ahithophel were sincere and really believed that they were speaking the "oracle of God." They were sincere but false, earnest but misled. Such prophets would have posed a serious problem to the most discerning hearer except for the fact that they were distinguishable by the God whose worship they advocated and not by their words, however sincere they proved to be. This is illustrated by the conflict in prophecy between Zedekiah ben Chennanah and Micaiah ben Inlah (I Kings 22:11-26). This fact is also illustrated by Hananiah and Jeremiah (Jer. 28).

In the second place, it is possible that what a preacher-prophet allows himself to hear through the Bible may be influenced by the situation in which he finds himself. If the situation is one which threatens his job or his life if he speaks forthrightly and honestly, he may allow himself to hear only those things in God's Word which will encourage some accommodation to the dominant voice being raised, which will permit some compromise with this voice, or which will permit him to be silent altogether. Thus God's voice may not be heard at all.

Admittedly the preacher-prophet stands in constant danger of this possibility against which he must always be on guard. But if he is true to his calling and to his God, when his personal integrity and that of his voice are at stake, he will choose rather to be in conflict with man than with God.

But how can the preacher-prophet know that when he speaks what he says is the Word of God? Are there any objective criteria by which he may know this? To be sure, there are. Let us list several of them.[4]

(1) When what the preacher-prophet says voices the characteristic and essential ideas of the Bible, he is an authentic spokesman for God. Those ideas will include the creative power, sovereignty, righteousness and holiness of God; the creatureliness and sinfulness of man, God's judgment upon sin and His redemption from sin through Jesus Christ; God's love

[4] The criteria submitted here are discussed quite fully and scholarly by John Knox in his book *The Integrity of Preaching*.

of man as his heavenly Father and man's love of man as his earthly brother; a community of justice and order and freedom on earth, and eternal life with God in the world to come.

These ideas are encountered so frequently and consistently in the Bible that they give the Bible its basic character. There is no mistaking whom the Old Testament sets forth as man's Creator and whom the New Testament sets forth as his Redeemer. The cause of man's fall in the Bible is too obvious to be gainsaid and the cause of his depravity too patent to be ignored. God's will for man in his social relationships and His design for man's earthly sojourn as a child of earth and a son of heaven are set forth in the Mosaic law, the teachings of the prophets, and in the life and teachings of Jesus and His apostles.

These ideas are so characteristic and dominant that they would not be difficult to recognize though the preacher-prophet presented them in the most modern of everyday speech, even though he did not announce a Biblical text before he began his message. For the authenticity of God's Word does not depend upon the announcement of a Biblical text or its conveyance through a certain, so-called "right" form of speech.

(2) The preacher-prophet may judge his authenticity as a spokesman of God by the contemporaneity or relevancy of his message. He must speak of the real needs of his times, not to what his contemporaries consider to be relevant for them. It must always be remembered that Jesus and His message have proved to be unquestionably relevant to the deepest needs of the people in His day but the "powers that be" crucified Him because they adjudged Him irrelevant. To be sure, He was irrelevant to their wants but not to their needs.

The authenticity of the preacher-prophet's message must be judged by what the Bible has to say concerning things of enduring value to man and by what man in his changing condition needs to have said to him for his saving health and peace, and not by what dying mass man wants to hear.

It is characteristic of contemporary man to want to hear what pleases him and what supports the status he has achieved and seeks to maintain with such tenacity. He likes comfort; therefore he resists anything which would disturb his ease. When he has made an adjustment to things as they are that is satisfactory to him, he does not desire or welcome change. He likes adulation and approval of what he does and what he considers important, and resents a disapproving judgment upon his decisions, choices, and accomplishments, especially when his deliberations and efforts have resulted in material progress and gain. It would seem to him in such circumstances that any voice which is critical or condemnatory of his achievements is a false and a foolish voice. Yet many times the preacher-prophet must be content with sounding foolish or even with being considered wrong in what he proclaims in the name of God. But this is a contentment growing out of his concern to be truly obedient and faithful in his delivery of the Word that God has given him to speak to the people. For man may be lost to God by the very success and prosperity which he attributes to the blessings of God but which are in fact only results of God's sufferance or of His judgment.

(3) The true preacher-prophet is distinguished by the God whose worship he advocates. If he advocates discord and hate, prejudice and sectional or narrow group interests; if he advocates disrespect for law and a partial administration of justice, the sufficiency of man and the adequacy of things, he is not an advocate of the worship of the God of our Lord Jesus Christ. For God is a God of justice and righteousness, and advocates of injustice and unrighteousness do not belong to Him. He is a God of love and mercy, and the apostle of hate, discord, and intolerance is no recipient of His counsel. He is a universal and eternal God, and no bigoted messengers of narrow, intolerant intellectual currencies can protest persuasively that they are sent by Him. They all may proclaim "Thus saith the eternal God" with their mouths, but their lives will demonstrate the deeds of the devil, their true master.

But he who with personal conviction and faith in his calling proclaims the saving deed of God in Christ Jesus our Lord, and calls men to a confession and repentance of their sins before God in Christ, is indeed a servant of the Word, committed to a redeeming and holy vocation. The purpose of his message is to turn the hearts of sinful, revengeful men to God, and to a ministry of reconciliation of man with his neighbor. For the heart so turned will find its fulfillment, its home, and its peace in God. And in finding these things, it loses the will to war with God, with itself, or with another. For this the true preacher-prophet aims. And to this end he gives himself in devotion and obedience to God's Word, whether this Word cuts between the marrow and the bone of the recalcitrant hearer or drops comfort as the still dew upon the ears of the troubled, wounded soul.

The true preacher-prophet advocates the worship of God who speaks in love and judgment to all men, and who wills that none of His children should be lost. He differs not in his treatment of either the rich or the poor, the strong or the weak, the socially acceptable or the outcast. The need of one soul is the object of His care. And beyond His love — or His judgment — no one can drift.

This God is a God of fire to His spokesman. The Word which He has placed in the mouth of His spokesman is itself a Word of fire, condemning and cleansing, and impelling the spokesman in the same way his own word condemns, cleanses, and incites to holy living those of his hearers who really hear. It comes with the force of many centuries to the mind of modern man, even with the poignancy and urgency of its first utterance to the Israelite clans in the desert.

Modern man in industrialized society may be hollow and empty, even dead, but he is not so dead that he is totally incapable of hearing the voice of the Son of man. And to those who hear the voice of God in mass society, it falls with the exposing power of an inward microscopic search. It reveals the secrets behind the deeds of the heart.

Men are made to face themselves so they may live — so they may live in obedience to the will of God. And to those who will not hear, the voice of God comes to haunt their sleep in every age through the necessity laid upon the true preacher-prophet to ask in God's name the searching and persistent question: Is the thing you do brotherly?

CHAPTER FIVE

The Word of God – with Imagination

The pastor of a large, metropolitan church spends his summer vacations "in the kind of travel which widens the horizons of the mind and enriches the experience of the heart." Last year he followed in the footsteps of an American giant – Abraham Lincoln. The pastor, guided and aided in his journey, to be sure, by his homiletical antenna, followed Lincoln from the Sinking Spring Farm at Hodgenville, Kentucky, where he was born, finally to Lincoln City in Spencer County, Indiana, where his mother, Nancy Hanks, died when he was nine years old. The tour ended at Spencer County. This tour had really been a "sight-seeing" tour. And the pastor had been able to *see* because he had purposed and taken the time *to look.*

But he had seen with more than his eyes. Because he had subjected himself to disciplined – and meditative or reflective – observation, he had also seen with his mind. For how true it is that "clear-eyed observation... profits the mind." Sight-seeing *and* mind-seeing were the two processes in which he was simultaneously involved. To look long, steadily, and precisely at an external fact is to experience the gradual formation of perceptions which lie behind the thing itself – perceptions which are the result of the mind seeing deeper meanings than the objectivity of the external fact.

Observation to this pastor included more than optical observation. He observed not only with his eyes but with his ears as well (listening). This is mental observation – having ears to hear. Likewise in this disciplined exercise there is a dual process at work: one hears the sound itself and listens to hear the deeper message of the sounds of one's sensory world.

> *Whether we look, or whether we listen,*
> *We hear life murmur, or see it glisten....*[1]

Observation of both kinds results in the achievement of imagination and is important to the preacher-prophet as a method of training the imagination. One learns to see precisely with the eye and mind and to feel responsibly with the heart. These are distinctly human achievements: perception which comes through mind-seeing and sympathy which comes through imagination. And the most precious yield of both is insight, which is a characteristic possession of the preacher-prophet.

The pastor in this discussion had set out deliberately to train his imagination and to discover insights into life, hence into the very raw material of preaching. His imagination, as he moved from place to place and from experience to experience with the child Lincoln, had become increasingly sharpened and in return had helped him to discover insights which were waiting for just such a person as he![2] One of the tangible things he brought back with him was the scribbled lines of a poem about Lincoln's mother which he discovered written on the wall of the souvenir shop at Knob Creek Farm. This poem illustrates the use of that kind of imagination which successfully meets the tests of both correspondence and coherence[3] and the achievement of sympathy — of feeling for and with another though he is far removed in time and space. The poem reads as follows:

---

[1] James Russell Lowell, *Vision of Sir Launfal,* Prelude to Part I, *Oxford Book of American Verse,* Bliss Carman, ed., Oxford University Press, 1927.

[2] It should be recognized that observation of a given thing, however well-disciplined it is, will not result in the same yields for all observers. What one sees will be conditioned by one's mental and emotional habits, one's experience, and the value system according to which external facts are observed and their internal meaning perceived.

[3] For an explanation of these philosophical terms see John Herman Randall, Jr., & Justus Buchler, *Philosophy: An Introduction,* Barnes & Noble Inc., 1942, pp. 133-135.

> *If Nancy Hanks*
> *Came back a ghost,*
> *Seeking news*
> *Of what she loved most,*
> *She'd ask first,*
> *"Where's my son?*
> *What's happened to Abe?*
> *What's he done?*
>
> *You wouldn't know*
> *About my son?*
> *Did he grow tall?*
> *Did he have fun?*
> *Did he learn to read?*
> *Did he get to town?*
> *Did you know his name?*
> *Did he get on?"*[4]

I

Not every preacher-prophet is endowed with the gift of creative imagination, albeit God has laid His hands upon him. He will need to work hard at developing effective skills. And his common experience will be that of getting results more by plodding with steady feet than by soaring with winged gifts. But to become responsibly imaginative in preaching is not beyond any preacher-prophet's grasp. To be sure, some will have more creative ability than others, a fact contingent upon a diversity of factors, but all can be trained to be more creative in imagination.

The writer has found it profitable in the training of his own imagination to return again and again to three written sources. He has made constant use of P. H. B. Lyons' delightful book *The Discovery of Poetry*.[5] Although it is a book on the appreciation of poetry, the methods employed toward this end have been found to be equally effective in learning how to see with the mind and feel with the heart as well as to listen with the ear. Its chapter on "Imagination" really prepares the conscientious reader for discovering not only the external world of poetry but

---

[4] Rosemary Benet, author.
[5] E. Arnold and Company, 1930.

the internal world as well. Besides, the book is rich in material which the most prolific preacher-prophet will find a treasury.

The second written source has been that of Henry David Thoreau's *Walden*. A perceptive naturalist, his observations on nature are not only fascinating and arresting but remarkably acute in perception and precise in detail. All of which are skills the man who would proclaim the Word of God needs to develop. His wit, apt phrase, spiritual insight, and descriptive detail would make any sermon sparkle when appropriately used and enrich the sermonic content. All of these are values in addition to the value of the training one receives in developing creative imagination. His description of "The Battle of the Ants" is instructive enough. But observe what reading about this battle does toward developing one's ability for mind-seeing when one reads Thoreau's comment on the battle. He remarks:

> I never learned which party was victorious, nor the cause of the war; but I felt for the rest of that day as if I had had my feelings excited and harrowed by witnessing the struggle, the ferocity and carnage, of a human battle before my door.[6]

A third written source has been children's literature, particularly *Childcraft*. Although the writer's thirteen-year-old daughter admonishes him that *Childcraft* is "for young children with limited comprehension," he has found it excellent for the training of the imagination. Particularly so are the interpretations of pictures by famous artists. They train both the eye and the mind to see.

The interpretation of Murillo's *The Divine Shepherd* is a case in point. It is a painting of the boy Jesus guarding His flock. Prominent in the painting is the child Jesus, with His shepherd's crook and His lamb. In the background of the painting, one may see the dim outlines of the rest of His flock. Behind the central figures of the child Jesus and the lamb is a broken pillar. Other ruins are in the foreground of the painting but are not too prominent. This is the pasture in which the child Jesus is guarding His sheep. This comment is made in the interpreta-

[6] Dodd, Mead, New York, 1946.

tion: "Perhaps the artist meant for the broken pillar to tell us that man-made things are more easily destroyed than faith and good deeds."[7] How suggestive this painting is!

There are, of course, many other written sources which may provide the preacher-prophet with excellent training in creative imagination — the writer has used some of them — but he has shown a preference for the three referred to here because of what they are capable of doing for him. But whatever written source can prove to be an appropriate and effective tool in the training of a given preacher-prophet's imagination should be employed fully and conscientiously by him. The result is the important thing.

II

There is another dimension to the training of the preacher-prophet's imagination. It lies in his training to preach the Word of God with imagination to contemporary man, the social product of mass production. Training the imagination must be geared to meeting the demands of communicating effectively with mass man. He is not more easily reached because of the availability of mass media of communication. This technological fact has rather increased the difficulty in communicating with him. He is more often talked to than communicated with.

The leanness of the soul of mass man contributes to the difficulty with which communication is carried on with him about spiritual things. His soul, like the clothing on his back, is mass-produced and is, therefore, lacking in deep spiritual sensitivity. Kenneth Fearing has penned a portrait of mass man to whom the Word of God must be preached with more than ordinary imagination:

> The clear brown eyes, kindly and alert, with 12-20 vision, give
>   confident regard to the passing world through R. K. Lampert
>   & Company lenses framed in gold;
> His soul, however, is all his own;
> Arndt Brothers necktie and hat (with feather) supply a touch
>   of youth.

[7] *Childcraft*, Field Enterprises Corp., Vol. 13, Art and Music, p. 10.

With his soul his own, he drives, drives, chats and drives,
The first and second bicuspids, lower right, replaced by bridge-
   work, while two incisors have porcelain crowns;

(Render unto Federal, state, and city Caesar, but not unto time;
Render nothing unto time until Amalgamated Death serves
   final notice, in proper form;

The vault is ready;
The will has been drawn by Clagget, Clagget, Clagget & Brown;
The policies are adequate, Confidential's best, reimbursing for
   disability, partial or complete, with double indemnity should
   the end be pure and simple accident)

Nothing unto time,
Nothing unto change, nothing unto fate,
Nothing unto you, and nothing unto me, or to any other known
   or unknown party or parties, living or deceased;
But Mercury shoes, with special arch supports, take much of
   the wear and tear;
On the course, a custombuilt driver corrects a tendency to slice;
Love's ravages have been repaired (it was a textbook case) by
   Drs. Schultz, Lightner, Mannheim, and Goode,
While all of it is enclosed in excellent tweed, with Mr. Baumer's
   personal attention to the shoulders and the waist;

And all of it now roving, chatting amiably through space in a
   Plymouth 6,
With his soul (his own) at peace, soothed by Walter Lippmann,
   and sustained by Haig & Haig.[8]

Mass, mass everywhere, is the trap of contemporary man. In
an anonymous parade of custom-made clothes and custom-built
cars, of body repairs and earthly securities, contemporary man
is moved on in a never-ending mass surge and sweep of "crowd
and machine life." Mass advertisement methods and harassment,
the overcoming pressures of an omnipotent salesmanship of
goods and services, of ideas and conformities, of credit cards and
causes have stupefied him. In this stupefaction he thinks (?)
that mass movement is real activity and crowd excitement is a
real pleasure. Living within the confines of a sensory world his

---

[8] Louis Untermeyer, ed., *Modern American Poetry*, Harcourt, Brace and
Co., 1950, p. 597.

soul is volatilized by mass movement and machine activity. He loses his soul happily in the belief that he is possessing it as his own.

This is what James Stevens recognizes in the conclusion of his article on "Detroit the Dynamic," although he expresses it in terms of the effect of the dynamics of Detroit upon himself as an outsider from a calmer, less massive community life:

> So much, and a hundred times more, I remember of Detroit as I muse away the hours in these quiet idle Hoosier woods. I yearn for the life there, somewhat as a retired man of the flying trapeze yearns for the big top, the parades, the crowds, the bands, the glitter and gauds of the circus. I must confess, however, that I ended my Detroit stay in a hospital. My golden town wore me out.[9]

This contemporary life situation, with its glitter, appeal, and efficiencies, and man's relation to it, imposes an enormous burden upon the imaginative powers of the preacher-prophet. His task is no simple proclamation of the Word. He must compete with a variety of mass-media attractions for even the attention of man today. He must be imaginative in preaching the Word of God in a way that men will be attracted to him and will want to hear him.

Moreover, his imaginative powers must plumb the depths of the condition of modern man and interpret to him his condition in concepts which will have meaning and attraction for him.[10]

III

Illustrative of this imaginative approach to the condition of man today is the reinterpretation of the concepts of sin and hell.

Sin, of course, is a Biblical concept but it is much more understandable to contemporary man when interpreted psychologically. This was the notable accomplishment of the Danish

[9] The *American Mercury*, November 1935.

[10] This is certainly possible as attested by the wide popularity a few decades ago of such a book as *Peace of Mind* and the wide currency of Dr. Vincent Peale's books. Whatever the deficiencies are in such books, the fact is, nevertheless, clear and convincing that religious literature and teaching can catch the imagination of men today, and many will be helped by the encounter.

philosopher-theologian Soren Kierkegaard. He treated sin as a psychological concept under the terms of "dread" and "despair." It is true that men were slow in comprehending these concepts when Kierkegaard first propounded them. But what thinking person today cannot understand through his own experience his dread of some indefinable something he knows not what and the difficulty and anguish he suffers in his need and attempts to relate himself to the self he was intended to be!

Since Kierkegaard there have been developed many variations on this main theme. Not the least impressive has been Tillich's discussion of sin in terms of man's estrangement from God, from his fellowman, and from himself.

He has this wise word to say:

> Man's predicament is estrangement, but his estrangement is sin. It is not a state of things, like the laws of nature, but a matter of both personal freedom and universal destiny. For this reason the term "sin" must be used after it has been reinterpreted religiously. An important tool for this reinterpretation is the term "estrangement."[11]

In non-theological-philosophical terms, Albert Camus has interpreted sin under the symbol of "the plague." This is a symbol which, in its suggestion of an infectious epidemic, mass man has no difficulty in understanding. About the individuality — and universality — of this plague, Camus has this comment to make:

> I know positively . . . that each of us has the plague within him; no one, no one on earth is free from it. And I know, too, that we must keep endless watch on ourselves lest in a careless moment we breathe in somebody's face and fasten the infection on him. What's natural is the microbe. All the rest — health, integrity, purity (if you like) — is a product of the human will, of a vigilance that must never falter.[12]

It has been the wisdom of modern interpreters of sin to start their discussions of the subject with men where they are — in the deep-felt awareness of their condition (of what is a problem or need to them, if you like). Estrangement is sin, but con-

---

[11] *Systematic Theology*, p. 46.
[12] *The Plague*, Knopf, 1948, p. 229.

temporary man must come to know what troubles him first of all as separation from himself, then from his fellow man, and ultimately from God. The use of the term sin can wait upon man's grasp of its reinterpretation.

The plague of an inward division or the lack of wholeness of the self is sin. But man must first comprehend his need for integration as the source of his personal and group difficulty and that it is only as a "new being" in Christ that the wholeness he needs may be achieved before he can really understand this plague to be sin.

Modern man's condition must be described to him first in the most natural terms as a prerequisite to his comprehension of its spiritual meaning.

IV

Hell is another concept which has undergone modern treatment and, consequently, is more comprehensible — and acceptable — to contemporary man.

The writer remembers with lingering vividness — and still some degree of embarrassment — the lesson taught him some years ago by an old unschooled pastor of a salt-mine congregation on Weeks Island in Louisiana. The congregation had gathered to hear the writer, then a young dean of a school of religion and an inexperienced holder of a doctor's degree, confident in his training. He does not remember now how the subject of hell was brought into his sermon, unless, of course, it was that being a good Baptist a warning against hell as the final abode of human souls was always in order. But he does remember that when he cried out the word hell, he pointed downward and the whole congregation was amused. The warning against hell did not have its desired result. It only served to undermine the little effect the young dean had been able to achieve up to this point.

When the service was over the pastor invited the speaker to accompany him on a tour of the salt mine. This tour led him down into the earth to a point where he came upon a crew of rough, callous, and vulgar men working and cursing and gambling, more than a thousand feet underground!

The old pastor was telling the young dean in a way which he would never forget that the underground concept of hell could never strike the imagination of men who were as much at home a thousand feet underground as they were on its surface. The young dean would have to be much more imaginative than he had been in his sermon if he really wanted to impress his hearers with the fear of hell.

A socio-psychological interpretation of hell is delineated by Lewis Mumford in his book *The Culture of Cities*.[13] He entitles one section of chapter four "A Brief Outline of Hell." The locus of hell is Megalopolis, the giant city of Western civilization. Perpetual economic unbalance, the necessity of a continuing war economy supported and sustained by a war psychology, the external conflicts and internal contradictions in a city which has become a "non-city" with its dwellers characterized by neurotic anxiety, is the state of hell described by Mumford. Hell for the mass-city dweller is a torturous entrapment in a situation of "barbarous mechanisms" and "mechanized barbarisms," producing dis-ease and futility. Alas! Megalopolis becomes Nekropolis, the city of decay and dead people.

This description of mass society men today will understand. However, it should be regarded by the preacher-prophet as only a beginning step and not a final one in a modern reinterpretation of hell. For hell is a religious concept and not simply a socio-psychological phenomenon.

Jean Paul Sartre is another contemporary writer who has been most imaginative in depicting hell for modern man. In his play, *No Exit*, he describes it as a drawing-room in Second Empire style with no mirrors, windows, or a bed. It is a room with a mantlepiece on which is a massive, monstrous-looking, immovable ornament. Three persons, a man and two women, are doomed to live together in this locked room without eyelids, hence no rest and sleep, but with memory and a "sense of human dignity," and with the lights in the room eternally on. There are no "instruments of torture," no "racks and red-hot pincers and

[13] Harcourt, Brace and Company, 1938, pp. 272 ff.

all the other paraphernalia." They discover that "there is no need for red-hot pokers." They are to be each other's torturers in a most ingenious sort of way, which is one of the high points of the play.[14] Hell has nowhere been more acutely depicted.

Whether interpreted socio-psychologically or theologically, hell must surely be viewed as a state of existence and a place. For there can be no state of existence without a structure of existence of which a state is its substance. The condition of hell delineated by Mumford found its locus in society, a social structure. The state of being in hell is interpreted by Sartre as people entrapped in a tormenting disrelationship with each other. Hell he described as a special kind of drawing-room. For he — an atheist! — bows to the logic of the need for a locus of such disrelationships. The existence of these disrelationships except in the entrapment of a specially prepared place would be an absurdity. Moreover, a closer view of Sartre's *No Exit* makes clear that he submits that each person had in his or her own pattern of life on earth both built and furnished this drawing-room.

We cannot argue definitely about the state and locus of hell after death, although we are acquainted with their reality here and now. But if we presuppose that personality is a reality beyond the grave, and that there shall be a continued existence of souls in the hereafter, we must accept the implication that consciousness and life will exist in some form. And it is this very *form* which suggests the particularization or an order of relationships of which the state is the substance, and its ability to sustain itself, the structure. This must be maintained whether the state of existence is good (heaven) or bad (hell).

V

Sin and *hell* are only two of the Biblical concepts which must be reinterpreted to mass man with finer, more appropriate imaginings. Grace and reconciliation, repentance and forgiveness, faith and obedience, and other Christian doctrines need to be made immediately intelligible and attractive to him. In making

[14] *No Exit* and *The Flies*, Knopf, 1946.

such concepts and doctrines intelligible and attractive, the preacher-prophet must be careful not to divest them of their Biblical content, but he must dress them in clothes suitable for a proper introduction to persons whom they should impress upon their first meeting and whose commitment they are to gain.

Mass men must be intrigued by the gospel message if they are to become its willing hearers. For to hear the Word is to receive it. And to receive it is to know eternal life. Therefore it is urgently important that the Word of God be delivered faithfully — and attractively, too!

CHAPTER SIX

The Word of God – with Conviction

It is more the truth of what the preacher-prophet *is* than of what he *says* which is communicated to his listeners. The things about which he is uncertain and which he has failed to make "visible rhetoric" in his own life are a further hindrance — added to other incumbrances — to the listeners' consent to believe. The very nature of the preaching ministry makes it necessary that the Word of God be preached with conviction if it is to encounter men as an issue of personal decision and choice. This conviction must be the spokesman's own personal conviction of the truth of the Word he proclaims and his personal faith in the ultimate fulfillment of its mission.

I

On the matter of personal conviction and faith, Frederick W. Robertson has left the preacher-prophet this reminder: It is not a minister's wisdom but his conviction which imparts itself to others. Nothing gives life but life, real flame alone kindles other flame; this was the power of the apostles: "We believe and therefore speak." Firm faith in what they spoke, that was the basis of the apostles' strength.[1]

The certainty of personal conviction is the *sine qua non* of

---

[1] *Sermons on St. Paul's Epistles to the Corinthians,* Ticknor and Fields, 1866, p. 303.

the preacher's effectiveness and the most efficacious conveyor of his message. For no mind or spirit communicates persuasively to other minds or spirits what it does not really believe and feel itself. Real communication of the gospel is the reception of truth felt and believed by him who speaks. If the preacher-prophet's message does not have this certainty, he is as a guide beckoning in the dark to others who have lost their way; he is as a fighter without a cause fighting monsters with sticks of straw. On the other hand, if his message imparts this certainty to others, men shall come to faith by faith in his belief and find their strength in the appropriation of his strength.

There is only one basis of this certainty — the apostolic basis announced in the words of Peter and John before the council after the healing of the lame man at the Gate Beautiful. They solemnly answered the council: "For we cannot but speak the things which we have seen and heard" (Acts 4:20). This must be true of the preacher-prophet today. Not only must the Word of God be authentic but his proclamation of the Word must likewise be authentic. It must be the proclamation of the saving deed of God in Jesus Christ which has become real in him. He must know the power and the glory of God's Self-disclosure to him not only as Creator and Redeemer but also as the Lord God of the prophets who has placed upon his heart a word to tell the people, and as the great Commissioner who has commissioned him to "preach the gospel to every creature" (Mark 16:15). In other words, of his conversion and his call to the Christian ministry there must be no doubt. For it must be against the background of these two primary Christian experiences that he must constantly declare the Word of God and interpret it to others.

The professional preparation which is demanded — and required — of the preacher-prophet today will not dull the acuteness of spiritual insight possessed by him who has experienced the saving grace of God and has been chosen by Him to be a messenger. Neither will his zeal and boldness be diminished. He will be disciplined but not languid, and literate without affectation. He will have an inquiring mind without being skeptical in attitude. He will be scholarly without being pedantic, serious without being soporific. Professional training he will regard as a part of the stewardship of preparation and the presentation of his best possible self as an offering to God who has entrusted him with the ministry of His Word.

At no time will he think that the methods and approaches and proximate, ascending steps in communicating the gospel to mass man in this discussion are so important as to be desirable ends in themselves. For they are not. He will view these things for what they really are: ways of encountering men in our technological civilization with the Word of God; he will be ministering to them in ways which will meet the demands of their contemporary condition. While various methods and techniques of communication are employed, he will not disregard the ministry of the Holy Spirit in and above what he contrives and the things which he does. While he presents to mass man proximate goals, he will not lose sight of the ultimate end to which his ministry calls him. He will have a passion for the salvation of the soul of mass man and the Christianization of the society of mass men.

All of this is an attitude of mind and disposition of spirit belonging to the man who has experienced a genuine conversion and a true call to the ministry of God's Word. Out of these experiences issue the certainty of his personal conviction concerning the Word of God and his illumination and inspiration for proclaiming it to others.

II

The preacher-prophet's certainty of conviction comprehends his personal faith in the ultimate fulfillment of the Word of God. He appreciates his role in the spiritualization of our common life and hence his contribution toward the fulfillment of the gospel's mission in this world. Daniel Webster has expressed what this role is as succinctly and acutely as anyone:

23096

Though we live in a reading age and in a reading community, yet the preaching of the Gospel is the form in which human agency has been and still is most efficaciously employed for the spiritual improvement of men.[2]

It has been suggested earlier that human instrumentality is God's best agency for making known His saving deed among men. But this human instrumentality must be specially chosen and qualified by God who chooses and sends men forth in the ministry of His Word. And every man thus chosen and qualified is under holy obligation to allow God's Word to prove its own power.

This is as Paul explains to the Corinthians what he was doing when he came to them with the gospel. He came to them "in fear, and in much trembling" with defective speech and an unimpressive body. But in spite of these natural handicaps, he adopted a manner of preaching the gospel which was quite unlike anything they were used to hearing from their popular and eminent orators. It would appear that Paul would have tried to compensate for his weakness and unimpressiveness with the employment of the clever, intriguing, and popular doctrines of the times presented with all of the oratory of which he was capable. But this he did not do. His method and manner were simply to declare the "testimony of God"; simply to witness to and personally to affirm the availability of salvation through "Jesus Christ, and him crucified." And this he did without "excellency of speech or of wisdom" of men. The proclamation and the way it was proclaimed were designed to show forth the excellency of the power of God.

This was the bold and daring approach of a man who had met God in Christ on the Damascus road and who had been captured to be a herald of the "good news" to all men. The certainty of his conviction made him bold and daring. His experience of Christ in conversion and in his call to the ministry of the Word gave him faith enough in the mission of God's Word to let it have free course through him. He believed the

[2] *The Complete Works of Daniel Webster,* Little, Brown and Company, 1903.

Word and dared to let it prove its power. This is how Paul puts it in his own words:

> And I, brethren, when I came to you, came not with excellency of speech or of wisdom, declaring unto you the testimony of God. And my speech and my preaching was not with enticing words of man's wisdom, but in demonstration of the Spirit and of power: That your faith should not stand in the wisdom of men, but in the power of God (I Cor. 2:1, 4-5).

The preacher-prophet must proclaim the Word under the conviction that its efficacy does not depend upon the employment of theatrics and eloquence for effect or the presentation of clever and intriguing topics of the day which in no way contribute to the salvation and edification of the soul. The Word of God proclaimed with conviction *is* power and will bring salvation to every one who will believe. And whether his hearers believe or not, they should at least be convinced that the preacher-prophet himself speaks from a firm conviction of the truth of what he proclaims; they should be convinced of his consciousness of the presence of Christ in the breaking of the "bread of life." It is said that upon persistent persuasion the English philosopher and historian, David Hume, wandered into the United Secession Church at Haddington to hear John Brown, one of the most effective and popular preachers in Scotland, who was stationed at this church for thirty-seven years. Hume sat through the sermon and admitted, when it was over: "That old man preaches as if Christ were at his elbow!" This was a skeptic's estimate of the preaching power of a humble man of God who had "picked up" his own education. But this was more than an estimate. It was a remarkable tribute to a spokesman who believed what he said and thus spoke with uncommon power.

Is not this the estimate for which every preacher-prophet should strive? Should not his greatest tribute be that he preaches "as if Christ were at his elbow"? If Christ is not there, he will not command the attention of the skeptic or send his ordinary hearers away "with a desire for, and an impulse toward, spiritual improvement." He will neither "fortify the feebleness of human resolution" nor "recall mankind from the bypaths where they turn into that broad path of salvation which all know, but few tread."

<h2 style="text-align:center">III</h2>

The results of the preacher-prophet, however, are not commensurate with his efforts. He is sometimes baffled and discouraged by the slow growth in enlightenment and spiritual improvement on the part of any conscientious and serious hearers of the Word. They show a discouraging lack of understanding and sympathy in crucial moments that demand a Christian maturity which, it is at length discovered, these hearers have never achieved. And yet for all their inadequacies and unevenness in spiritual growth they at other times demonstrate an amazing spiritual sensitivity and devotion which is difficult to explain except in terms of the action of the Word through the Holy Spirit who works above what man himself is able to accomplish. One can hardly imagine that the venom and acrimony with which Augustus M. Toplady attacked John Wesley could have come from the same heart and mind that gave to the Church one of its tenderest prayer hymns:

> *Rock of Ages, cleft for me,*
> *Let me hide myself in Thee;*
> *Let the water and the blood,*
> *From Thy riven side which flowed,*
> *Be of sin the double cure:*
> *Cleanse me from its guilt and power.*

> *Not the labors of my hands*
> *Can fulfil Thy law's demands;*
> *Could my zeal no respite know,*
> *Could my tears forever flow,*
> *All for sin could not atone;*
> *Thou must save, and Thou alone.*

> *Nothing in my hand I bring,*
> *Simply to Thy cross I cling;*
> *Naked, come to Thee for dress,*
> *Helpless, look to Thee for grace;*
> *Foul, I to the fountain fly;*
> *Wash me, Saviour, or I die.*

> *While I draw this fleeting breath,*
> *When my eyelids close in death,*
> *When I soar to worlds unknown,*
> *See Thee on Thy judgment-throne,*
> *Rock of Ages, cleft for me,*
> *Let me hide myself in Thee.*[3]

Now contrast with "Rock of Ages" the vituperations of this Calvinistic preacher and hymn writer against the aged Arminian John Wesley who had remained comparatively silent in the raging controversy over antinomianism. Toplady bitterly referred to John Wesley as "an old Fox tarred and feathered"; "a designing wolf"; "the most perfect and holy and sly that e'er turned a coat, or could pilfer and lie"; "a dealer in stolen wares, as unprincipled as a rock and as silly as a jackdaw"; "a gray-headed enemy of all righteousness": "a venal profligate"; "an apostate miscreant"; "the most rancorous hater of the Gospel system that ever appeared in this land"; "a low and puny tadpole in divinity."[4] And in his last illness Toplady announced that if he were on his death-bed with a pen in hand he "would not strike out a single line" of what he had written about John Wesley and his beliefs.

This classic illustration sets forth in bold relief the ambitendency of hearers and doers of the Word, of committed Christians. This ambitendency taxes one's faith in the effectiveness of the Word received by another. Certainly the faithful hearers and servants of God's Word must often pain the heart of the preacher-prophet by their external expressions of this inner fact. Is he, because of this, to declare with correspondingly weakened conviction the power of the Word to transform and to redeem? Is he justified in losing faith in the genuine and stable spiritual improvement of *any* man? What shall he think of the Christian

---

[3] Quoted from *The Methodist Hymnal*, The Methodist Book Concern, 1905, p. 196; hymn altered. Published in this form in *The Gospel Magazine* for March, 1776. Quoted from Louis F. Benson, *Studies of Familiar Hymns* (Second Series), The Westminster Press, 1923, p. 104.

[4] Quoted from *John Wesley the Methodist*, by a Methodist Preacher, The Methodist Book Concern, 1903, p. 207. See also *Studies of Familiar Hymns* (Second Series), pp. 108-117.

conviction and experience of individuals who invariably lower their standard of personal morality to conform to the standard of the group? Is the power of the Word operative at all in the internal contradictions of our personal and group life? What is its witness?

These and other such questions tax the certainty of the preacher-prophet's conviction of the power of the Word he preaches but without this certainty he would find it impossible to transcend the discouragement and lack of promise man's ambitendency so often presents.

Many anomalies and inconsistencies evident in the life and conduct of professing Christians who are nurtured regularly on the Word of God would be unbearable perplexities except for the conviction that God works, in spite of man as well as through him, to fulfill the mission of His Word. The preacher-prophet must declare the Word of God under this conviction lest he become discouraged by the slow spiritual improvement of those whom he would inspire with a desire to be more like their Lord Jesus Christ. This conviction is Biblical and the preacher-prophet's must be rooted in the Bible. He may find in Isaiah a source of this certainty of conviction about the mission of the Word of God:

> For as the rain cometh down, and the snow from heaven, and returneth not thither, but watereth the earth, and maketh it bring forth and bud, that it may give seed to the sower, and bread to the eater: so shall my word be that goeth forth out of my mouth: it shall not return unto me void, but it shall accomplish that which I please, and it shall prosper in the thing whereto I sent it (Isa. 55:10-11).

The Word proclaimed in one form has its fruition in another. It is delivered as spoken word and returned as "lived speech" wherever it is received in faith; its fruition is in a divinely inspired life and dedicated, though sometimes misconceived, service.

As there is a waiting time between the falling of the rain or the melting of the snow and the feeding of the nether growth until it comes at last to full fruition above the soil, so there is a time of waiting between the sowing of the Word in the hearts of men, its hidden growth, and its harvest. And what this harvest will be depends upon the soil or condition of heart upon which the Word falls.

This period of waiting is a time of special activity of the Holy Spirit, operating as it does in such times between the end of man's effort and the beginning of its patent results. The herald has now reached the boundary of his planting activity and the fulfillment of his mission. He must now hope and wait in faith upon the outcome of his labors. The serious and truly spiritually hospitable hearer of the Word now experiences the Holy Spirit's invasion of his soul — His invasion of the borders of his personal consent and his reception of the Word. And under the quickening and nurturing power of the Spirit, the hearer begins his slow ascent to the higher life of a new creature in Christ Jesus.

The mission of the Word is not conditioned by the state of the hearer's heart. Whether the Word is gladly received or roundly rejected, it is never proclaimed without purpose or effect. To be sure, the effect may be positive or negative. As a positive effect, the Word evokes a congenial and holy response from its hearers. The Word as a pronouncement of judgment upon the unresponsive heart is its negative effect. Thus the Word goes forth in hope and judgment, to redeem and reconcile, to warn and to condemn. It shall not return empty and spent to God from whom it has gone forth. It shall not ultimately betray the faith and confidence of him who has proclaimed it. Neither shall it fail in its ministries to men. The longing soul it shall satisfy and the hungry soul it shall fill with goodness. It shall be to them who thirst living water and to the rich as well as the poor bread without price. There shall be established between those who hear and the God whose Word is spoken "an everlasting covenant, even the sure mercies of David" which will herald and accomplish the release of the soul of man from its modern, satanic captivity and nourish the growth of a kingdom of love which is a kingdom of authentic selves.

Isaiah concludes his prophecy of the fulfillment of the mission of the Word in a notable manner to the captive Jews:

> For ye shall go out with joy, and be led forth with peace: the mountains and the hills shall break forth before you into singing, and all the trees of the field shall clasp their hands. Instead of the thorn shall come up the fir tree, and instead of the brier shall come up the myrtle tree; and it shall be to the Lord for a name, for an everlasting sign that shall not be cut off (Isa. 55:12-13).

The prophet Isaiah begins his prophecy on a note of hope and promise and ends it on a note of exultation. This, likewise, should be the way the preacher-prophet today begins and ends his ministry of the Word of God. He seldom has difficulty beginning his ministry with hope and promise for the Word he proclaims or for himself and the role he will play in the fulfillment of the mission of the Word. But the increasing harassment and exigencies of his ministry do not always leave him with a sense of accomplishment or in a mood of exultancy. He is often too preoccupied with the little discouragements and defeats in the daily skirmishes of his life and work to have a vision of victory of the outcome of the whole spiritual struggle on earth. When the preacher-prophet comes to this state of affairs in his own life and ministry, it is past time for him to withdraw "far from the madding crowd's ignoble strife" and to rediscover those sources of conviction, illumination, and inspiration which inspired him in the beginning to a noble, courageous, and confident ministry of the Word of God.

For all men in mass society today, the preacher-prophet must be alive, vibrant with hope and confidence, genuine in his role, and strong enough with a firm faith in the Word he preaches, to be "the voice of one crying in the wilderness" of our mass-produced society, a seeker of estranged souls in the market place of Unreal City, a hope-giving companion to lost souls on the lonely roads of doubt and despair, and a source of substance and enrichment to "hollow men" seeking to be authentic selves in "the waste land" of contemporary mass society. He must be an authentic spokesman for God. His voice must be a voice of conviction to men who are yet indifferent; it must proclaim the Word of life to men who are dying for lack of *something* to capture their imaginations — and their souls. His faith must be a haven for the faithless hearts of others so that those who will to believe may believe in his belief. What more arresting portrait can we find of what the preacher-prophet should be today in mass society than that which is given of a man belonging to the Kingdom of God in the book of Isaiah!

And a man shall be as an hiding place from the wind, and a covert from the tempest; as rivers of water in a dry place, as the shadow of a great rock in a weary land. And the eyes of them that see shall not be dim, and the ears of them that hear shall hearken (Isa. 32:2-3).

So let the preacher-prophet be today!

BIBLIOGRAPHY

Babbage, Stuart Barton, *Man in Nature and in Grace.* Grand Rapids, Michigan: Wm. B. Eerdmans Publishing Company, 1957.

Barry, F. R., *Recovery of Man.* New York: Charles Scribner's Sons, 1949.

Benet, Rosemary, *Poem* (title and publisher unknown).

Benson, Louis F., *Studies of Familiar Hymns* (Second Series). Philadelphia: Westminster Press, 1923.

Browning, Robert, *The Complete Poetic and Dramatic Works.* New York: Houghton Mifflin Company, 1895.

Brunner, Emil, *Man in Revolt.* Philadelphia: Westminster Press, 1947.

Buber, Martin, *Between Man and Man.* New York: The Macmillan Company, 1947.

Camus, Albert, *The Plague.* New York: Knopf, 1948.

Childcraft, Vol. 13. Chicago: Field Enterprises Educational Corporation.

Cowan, Wayne H. (ed.), *What The Christian Hopes for in Society.* New York: Association Press, 1957.

Cowper, William, *The Task,* Book 2, in *A Book of English Literature,* F. B. Snyder and R. G. Martin (eds.), rev. F. B. Snyder. New York: The Macmillan Company, 1933.

Donne, John, excerpt from *Devotions,* in *Complete Poetry and Selected Prose of John Donne* and *Complete Poetry of William Blake,* John Hayward and Geoffrey Keynes (eds.). New York: Random House, 1941.

Eliot, T. S. *Christianity and Culture.* New York: Harcourt, Brace and Company.

Eliot, T. S., *The Idea of a Christian Society.* New York: Harcourt, Brace and Company, 1949.

Eliot, T. S., *Collected Poems.* New York: Harcourt, Brace and Company, 1930.

Ferris, Theodore Parker, *Go Tell the People.* New York: Charles Scribner's Sons, 1951.

Heidegger, Martin, *Existence and Being.* Chicago: Henry Regnery Company, 1950.

Kierkegaard, Soren, *The Sickness Unto Death.* New York: Princeton University Press, 1941; Reprinted, A Doubleday Anchor Book.

Kierkegaard, Soren, excerpt from *Concluding Unscientific Postcript,* in *A Kierkegaard Anthology,* Robert Bretall (ed.). New York: Princeton University Press, 1946.

Knox, John, *The Integrity of Preaching*. Nashville: Abingdon Press, 1957.

Lee, E. G., *Mass Man and Religion*. New York: Harper and Brothers, 1949.

Longfellow, Henry Wadsworth, *Tales of a Wayside Inn*.

Lowell, James Russell, *The Vision of Sir Launfal*, Part I. *Oxford Book of American Verse*. London: Oxford University Press.

Ludwig, Emil, *The Nile*. New York: Viking Press, 1938.

Lyons, P. H. B., *The Discovery of Poetry*. London: E. Arnold & Company, 1930.

Mennonite Hymnary. Berne, Indiana: Mennonite Book Concern, 1940.

Methodist Preacher, A, *John Wesley the Methodist*. New York: The Methodist Book Concern, 1903.

Mounce, Robert H., *The Essential Nature of New Testament Preaching*. Grand Rapids, Michigan: Wm. B. Eerdmans Publishing Company, 1960.

Mumford, Lewis, *The Culture of Cities*. New York: Harcourt, Brace and Company, 1938.

Niebuhr, Reinhold, *The Nature and Destiny of Man*, Volume 2. New York: Charles Scribner's Sons.

Park, Robert Ezra, *The Free Press*, 1950.

Phillips, J. B., *The New Testament in Modern English*. New York: Macmillan Company, 1952.

Randall, Jr., John Herman and Justus Buchler, *Philosophy: An Introduction*. New York: Barnes and Noble, Inc., 1942.

Robertson, F. W., *Sermons on St. Paul's Epistles to the Corinthians*. Boston: Ticknor and Fields, 1866.

Sartre, Jean-Paul, *No Exit* and *The Flies*. New York: Knopf, 1946.

Spengler, Oswald, *Decline of the West*. New York: Knopf, 1926.

Stevens, James, "Detroit the Dynamic," *The American Mercury*, November, 1935.

The Holy Bible, Revised Standard Version. New York: Thomas Nelson and Sons, 1952.

The Methodist Hymnal. New York: The Methodist Book Concern, 1905.

Thoreau, Henry David, *Walden*. New York: Dodd, Mead, 1946.

Tillich, Paul, *The Courage To Be*. New Haven: Yale University Press, 1952; *Systematic Theology*, Volume 2. Chicago: The University of Chicago Press, 1957.

Tonnies, Ferdinand J., *Gemeinschaft und Gesellschaft*, 1897.

Toynbee, Arnold J., *A Study of History*, abridgement of vols. 1-6 by D. C. Somervell. London: Oxford University Press, 1946.

Untermeyer, Louis (ed.), *Modern American Poetry*. New York: Harcourt, Brace and Company, 1950.

Wallis, Louis, *Sociological Study of the Bible*. Chicago: University of Chicago Press, 1912.

Webster, Daniel, *The Complete Works of Daniel Webster*. New York: Little, Brown and Company, 1903.

Indexes

INDEX OF PRINCIPAL SUBJECTS

INDEX OF PROPER NAMES

INDEX OF SCRIPTURAL REFERENCES